MARY SACHS

MERCHANT PRINCESS

BARBARA TRAININ BLANK

SUNBURY
PRESS

Mechanicsburg, PA USA

Published by Sunbury Press, Inc.
105 South Market Street
Mechanicsburg, Pennsylvania 17055

SUNBURY
P R E S S

www.sunburypress.com

For information about special discounts for bulk purchases, please contact Sunbury Press Orders Dept. at (855) 338-8359 or orders@sunburypress.com.

To request one of our authors for speaking engagements or book signings, please contact Sunbury Press Publicity Dept. at publicity@sunburypress.com.

ISBN: 978-1-62006-645-4 (Hard cover)

Library of Congress Control Number: 2015957315

FIRST SUNBURY PRESS EDITION: November 2015

Product of the United States of America
0 1 1 2 3 5 8 13 21 34 55

Set in Bookman Old Style
Designed by Crystal Devine
Cover by Lawrence Knorr
Edited by Allyson Gard

Continue the Enlightenment!

CONTENTS

Foreword (Original)......................................vii

Author's Note (Original) ix

Author's Note (This Edition).......................xi

Acknowledgments......................................xiii

Street Renamed 1

Who Was Mary Sachs? In Brief.................. 6

Historical Background............................ 11

The Origins 16

The Stores.. 24

The Woman 50

Reading Matter and Interests.................... 75

The Broader View 76

The Legacy 79

The Charitable Instinct............................ 84

Epilogue... 90

Downtown Harrisburg during the Tenure
    of Mary's Store 93

Mary Remembered................................... 95

Appendices

    Appendix I 97

    Appendix II 100

    Appendix III 101

Additional Bibliography 102

MARY SACHS: MERCHANT PRINCESS

"She opened her own store and it became a symbol of retail sophistication and glamor. She was an epitome of style and substance."

—Historical Society of Dauphin County web site

FOREWORD (ORIGINAL)

For 75 years in Central Pennsylvania, the name "Sachs" represented quality and originality in business, generosity and creativity in philanthropy, and selflessness and hard work in community service.

Mary Sachs, the Merchant Princess of Pennsylvania, and her two sisters, Hannah Sachs Cantor in Harrisburg and Yetta Sachs Carpenter in Lancaster, symbolized the very best of the American spirit during their long lives. They set an example for their large and extended family, which continues through their descendants and most conspicuously is carried forward by the charitable trusts established by Mary Sachs in 1961 and Hannah Sachs Center in 1999.

While Mary Sachs was the matriarch of three generations of the Sachs family, she never married but became and remained the heart and soul of a large family that continues to serve the needy and the less fortunate of all backgrounds in Central Pennsylvania. She had two very close helpmates throughout her life and business career, her sisters Yetta and Hannah.

We of the fourth generation of the Sachs family in America have continued that tradition and have individually established scholarships and other philanthropies, which have in their own way derived directly from the example of our aunts Mary, Hannah, and Yetta.

This story is a reminder of how very difficult life was a century ago for penniless Jewish immigrants. It is an inspiration for all, in that it demonstrates how hard work and willpower provide almost immediate success in our beloved country. It is also a warning that eternal vigilance in the form of charity and encouragement of self-help for the poor, needy, and sick are the best assurance of a successful American republic.

We are proud of our family heritage and, motivated by the example of Mary, Hannah, and Yetta, look to the future knowing that the people of Central Pennsylvania will benefit forever from their work and philanthropy. We also know that others elsewhere will follow that path of generosity of spirit that has made America a great and truly free leader among the nations of the world.

—William S. Greenberg, Chair
Mary Sachs Trust, Washington, D.C.

Author's Note (Original)

Ever since Sir Isaac Newton attributed his scientific insights to "standing on the shoulders of giants" some four centuries ago, communities have used the phrase to remind present generations how much they owe to the contributions of those who have gone before.

It may be a cliché today, but it is nevertheless true. Especially so for those who not only succeeded and contributed in their own times but also for the true giants who then left assets to enhance the lives of future generations they would never know.

In Central Pennsylvania the names of Mary Sachs and two of her sisters, Hannah Sachs Cantor and Yetta Sachs Carpenter, have earned a place on that roster of past giants.

Their saga reflects upon several elements of American history—immigrant contributions to our economy and society despite hardships, achievements in business, contributions to the Jewish community, and the role of women in the United States.

To record and remember their story does more than pay proper respect to the memory of these people. It can serve to inspire our own generation to be aware of the importance of thinking of our future and about the vital role charity can play in making this a better place in which to live beyond our own lifetimes.

Thanks are due to the friends, relatives, and acquaintances of Mary Sachs, who were most generous with their time and memories; to grand-nephew Jeffrey Jacobs, who made Hannah Sachs Cantor's papers available; and to the professionals at the State Archives and Dauphin County Historical Society, who shared their compilations of Mary Sachs's letters, papers, oral history recordings, and clippings.

Special thanks are due also to Frances Goldberg and her late husband, attorney Arthur Goldberg, who first suggested this project more than a half decade ago; to the members of the Mary Sachs Charitable Trust; to Hannah's trust officer and dear friend, Christopher W. Kull of Sterling Financial Trust in Lancaster; and to Hannah's attorney, Neil E. Hendershot of Goldberg, Katzman & Shipman in Harrisburg, who fathered this project to completion. Morton Spector's assistance in the final stages of this project is greatly appreciated.

An expression of gratitude also goes to the institutions named in the trust established by Hannah Cantor in her will—Elizabethtown College, Hadassah, the Hospice of Central Pennsylvania, Dickinson College, Gettysburg College, the United Jewish Community of Greater Harrisburg, the Rabbi David L. Silver Yeshiva Academy, the United Jewish Appeal, the Jewish Community Center of Harrisburg, the Jewish Home of Greater Harrisburg, Lebanon Valley College, Harrisburg Area Community College, and the American Associates of Ben Gurion University—without whose participation this volume might not exist.

Finally, this fragmentary history of their achievements in business and in communal charity is dedicated to the memory of Mary and Hannah, whom I knew casually in life but now know better, and to the memory of Yetta, whose efforts and personality I came to appreciate during months of research.

—Bern Sharfman, June 2003

Author's Note (This Edition)

My acquaintanceship with the legacy and memory of Mary Sachs began in 1991, two years after my husband and I had moved to Harrisburg. That was also the same year our younger daughter was born. We began to use the day-care center at the Jewish Community Center and became familiar with the building and campus.

We also became familiar with the Auditorium of the JCC—named for Mary—and with the compelling portrait of her that hangs on one of its walls. My children thought that, like the Mona Lisa, Mary Sachs's eyes were following them. At first, to be honest, we didn't really connect with who Mary was, but gradually learned more from hearing people speak about her all the time and from the little glass case in the entranceway to the Auditorium containing photos of her and some memorabilia.

My curiosity was further whetted when I became friendly with Frances Goldberg, one of the leading citizens and philanthropists of Jewish Harrisburg. She in turn introduced me to Hannah Sachs Cantor, one of Mary's sisters. Hannah had managed the store after Mary's passing, and then sold it to Hess's (a fact, as this manuscript indicates later, she then regretted). Hannah plied me with chocolate kisses for my children—she and her husband, Ben, did not have any kids of their own—and told me volumes about her sister.

Hannah wanted Bern Sharfman, the original author of this book who lived in her building, to write about Mary. It was no secret that Hannah adored and idolized her older sister and that the two were very close. It was only after

Hannah's passing that Bern began to write the book, sensing, correctly, I think, that Hannah was interested in a book that would make Mary out to be a paper saint. In other words, hagiography.

I was touched, though, when Jeff Jacobs, one of Mary and Hannah's great-nephews, told me that before her passing Hannah had indicated a desire for me to come and take clothes out of her closet. I did take a few things. One was a wonderful red wool skirt with black and gold embroidery, which had a Mary Sachs label. That made it very special, indeed. (Unfortunately, I "outgrew" the skirt size-wise.)

Jeffrey also shared with me a cache of Mary's letters and other papers, which I passed on to Bern.

Many years later, not long before we moved away from Harrisburg, in fact, I was meeting with Lawrence von Knorr of Sunbury Press about another book of mine he considered publishing. (The book, which was released in November 2013, is about caregiving.)

Being a great lover of history and biography, Larry asked if there was anyone in the Jewish community of Harrisburg who hadn't gotten his or her due in writing. Mary's name came to my lips immediately, despite the fine book Bern had written. I thought perhaps there was more to say. Larry was fascinated—and surprised she wasn't better known today.

The board of the Mary Sachs Trust agreed that more might be said about Mary's business acumen and the main focus of this new revised book (that Mr. Knorr agreed to) should really be on her entrepreneurial success as an individual, rather than on her extensive and impressive acts of tzedakah, or philanthropy.

So this book was born.

—Barbara Trainin Blank

ACKNOWLEDGMENTS

Thanks are due to Larry and his wife and business partner, Tammi, and to Sunbury Press; to the Trust; and to the staff of the Pennsylvania State Archives, the Historical Association of Dauphin County, and the Historic Harrisburg Association. Thanks also to my family, friends, and acquaintances who heard more about Mary Sachs during the writing of this book than they had ever anticipated. (Many, in fact, had not heard of her before—another reason to write this book.)

And of course, my gratitude and esteem go to Bern, may he rest in peace, a unique storyteller, a writer of grace and humor, and a warm, distinctive personality, without whose initial substantial efforts this book would not have been possible.

There is one more person, also no longer with us, I would like to acknowledge. That is my father, Rabbi Isaac N. Trainin, who, like Mary, came from Eastern Europe as a child (although he was older than she was at the time of immigration), He grew up in a family with few economic resources but was blessed with a great deal of ambition and vision. Like Mary, he accomplished a great deal in his chosen field—Jewish social service and philanthropy. To him and to my mother, his worthy helpmeet, Frances Schneider Trainin, are due much love and gratitude.

Special thanks as well to Morton Spector, liaison to the Trust, whose energy and devotion to every task at hand are exceptional.

"Between the time research was conducted for this book and the time of publication, some of the people who were then alive may have since been deceased. Our apologies for any such unavoidable "errors."

Street Renamed

It was a beautiful fall day. Friday, October 5, 2012. Dignitaries had gathered, as had members of the board of the Mary Sachs Trust. Curious pedestrians passed by, some asking what was going on. Some were aware there had been a fashionable clothing store started on that block by Mary Sachs. Others were not. Usually, those in the latter group were young.

Morton Spector, advisor to the Trust, chaired the proceedings, and the speakers included then-Mayor Linda Thompson.

What was the special occasion? The stretch of North Third Street in Harrisburg between Locust and Pine Street had been, not renamed, but given an additional name—the Mary Sachs Way. This renaming honored the woman who had once been synonymous with entrepreneurship, style, and grace in fashion.

An immigrant without formal education, she had overcome adversity, including a fire that felled her first store, to become one of Harrisburg's most successful and prestigious citizens.

The event honored another side of Mary Sachs—a woman as famous for her charitable activities as for her elegant clothing stores. This legacy has been kept alive by the Mary Sachs Trust—although Sachs herself had passed away on May 22, 1960, at the age of 72 of cancer.

Also speaking that day was Ben Wielebinski, a staff member of the New Birth of Freedom (Boy Scouts of America) Council. He acknowledged Mary Sachs's contribution to the organization years earlier in giving the donation that enabled the purchase of land for a Boy Scout's camp, which came to be known as Hidden Valley Scout Reservation.

Although many of Mary's charitable activities were directed toward Jewish causes, she supported a wide array of organizations.

Later in the day, the members of the Trust and guests walked to Strawberry Square, a large indoor mall a block or so away in downtown Harrisburg, where display cases contained an exhibit dedicated to Mary Sachs. Appropriately, the exhibit was located across from Dress Barn.

The exhibit continued till the end of the month, and had been assembled and put together by the Historical Society of Dauphin County—which is one of the repositories in the city of a Mary Sachs collection.

Another is the Pennsylvania State Archives.

The exhibit covered some of the highlights of Sachs's life and career:

- How she bought a 28-acre plot near Loysville, Perry County, as a boy scouts' camp she intended to be named for her good friend, Rabbi Philip David Bookstaber, spiritual leader of Temple Ohev Sholom.
- How she contributed to Ohev Sholom's Sunday School, but stipulated that it be open to non-members (her parents were Orthodox).
- She was a Founding contributor to the Albert Einstein College of Medicine of Yeshiva University in New York.
- She was active in the National Conference of Christians and Jews.
- Mary met Eleanor Roosevelt at a UJCA campaign dinner in Harrisburg; the two became friends, and Roosevelt mentioned Mary in "My Day," her column.
- There was a "Sachs Army": Mary hosted up to 18 students at a time of the Air Force Intelligence School during World War II, reserving a small part of the house for her own living quarters.

- Michael Comay, chief delegate of Israel to the United Nations in the 1960s and a leading diplomat, honored Mary at a 1959 event with a pin, entitled "First Woman of Valor."
- Architect Eleanor Le Maire designed both the interior of the store on North Third Street. as well as Mary's home. The March 1936 issue of *The Architectural Record* featured scenes from the store.

But, of course, Mary Sachs was primarily about fine clothing and elegance. In the exhibit were items that belonged to a number of central Pennsylvania luminaries: the white satin wedding gown worn by Eleanor Martin, when she married Heath Allen; a cocktail dress of Bertha May Taylor, wife of Harvey, the Pennsylvania State Senator and GOP leader; two outfits owned by Alyce Spector, community leader and wife of Morton Spector; and outfits of Richard Abrams, from the 212 Men's Shop that was part of the Mary Sachs store complex.

At the time of the height of Mary's career as a clothier, there were maybe 5000 Jews in Harrisburg—most of whom had retail businesses, such as Goldsmith's furniture, and Kaufman's Department Store. The Mary Sachs store started with a full ladies' department store and expanded into men's, shoes, china and silver, and gifts. The second floor offered couture clothing.

While there were other women who owned businesses, Mary's may have had the greatest reach both in and outside Harrisburg.

Mary's store was, Alyce Spector said, a "store of elegance. There was no other store like it, except in New York. Mary duplicated Saks Fifth Avenue and Bergdorf Goodman and elegant jewelry stores like Winston."

Reportedly, someone once asked Mary why she didn't put a store on New York's Fifth Avenue, and she jokingly replied: "I will if Bergdorf Goodman lets me."

Aside from Eleanor Roosevelt, among the prominent people Mary befriended were the Eisenhowers; Mamie was a devoted customer.

Due in large part to Mary Sachs, Harrisburg became noted as being in the top percentile for raising money for Jewish causes for the size of the community, Spector added.

Mary Sachs became synonymous not with fickle fashion but with long-lasting quality. Spector still has at least one outfit from the store she still wears—a plaid mohair skirt and stole. But she also bought her trousseau to go away from there.

"It was very elegant and very upscale," Spector said of the store. "They were all magnificent fabrics, all designer clothes, higher priced than regular clothes. Clothes then [in general] weren't so spiffy."

In addition to members of the Jewish population, a lot of politicians and other notables would come to the store. "Mary Sachs sent packages to DC, Texas, all over the place," she recalled.

An earlier exhibit assembled by the Historical Society in 2007 was entitled: "Mary Sachs, The Epitome of Style and Substance."

The 2007 exhibit featured selected Mary Sachs clothing and accessories donated or loaned to the Society by local residents who never forgot the uniqueness of the Mary Sachs retailing experience. Also on display was a large-scale photograph reproduction of the Mary Sachs Harrisburg storefront as it existed after World War II, as well as photographs documenting her lifelong commitment to family and community.

In an article in the Sunday *Patriot-News* of March 25, 2007, about the exhibit that year, columnist Mary O. Bradley called the Mary Sachs shop a "pearl in the necklace of fine apparel and jewelry stores along fashionable North Third Street."

Bradley in turn quoted Beatrice Hulsberg, guest curator for the exhibit: "Mary Sachs was such a tremendous leader in retail fashions. She was internationally known and trend setting insofar as she treated her customers and her store design. Her customers were important to her."

The Historical Society also sponsored an earlier exhibit, in 1990. To prepare for this exhibit, the Dauphin County Historical Society ran a tiny notice in the newspaper requesting clothing that had been purchased from one of the Mary Sachs shops. In two weeks, the society received more than 250 offers.

A "procession" of wedding gowns from the 1940s to the 1960s revealed the world-class fashion sense and eye for quality that Sachs brought to Harrisburg, noted Elaine Hermann in the *Central Penn Business Journal.* "Sachs' name," she added, often made the columns of *Women's Wear Daily* and other leading fashion industry publications. But it was the retailing concept she created that fixed her name in international fashion world history.

When Mary was interviewed in 1942 about opening her own store, she said: "When one has no job, one must do something, so I went into business," despite being, in Bradley's words, "long on initiative and short on cash."

The original shop, which opened on September 6, 1918, consisted of two stock rooms and six fitting rooms, but Mary described it in an advertisement as "a little piece of Fifth Avenue."

In a 1943 interview, Mary said: "I believe in fine clothes, and by that I do not mean the most expensive or the most extreme styles. I mean the finest quality of line and material and those dateless styles which will give service and pleasure through many seasons."

Hulsberg, Guest Curator of the 2007 Historical Society of Dauphin County, further commented that although some of the apparel in the exhibit was 50 years old, "the quality of the fabrics and construction is exceptional."

WHO WAS MARY SACHS? IN BRIEF

Born on March 10, 1888, Mary Sachs was a Russian-born immigrant who was only four years old when she came to America (in 1892) with her mother, Fanny Rhoads Sachs, and two siblings, Sarah and Emma. The family found husband and father Wolf Sachs in Renovo, a town in the lumber and coal region of northern Pennsylvania. Wolf Sachs was a peddler and shop owner who had immigrated four years before the rest of his family.

Around 1900, the Sachs family moved to Baltimore, where Lena, Esther, Morris, Yetta, and Hannah were born. Mary called Morris, her only brother, the "long-awaited kadishel," referring to the fact that it is the son who is required by Jewish tradition to recite the Kaddish prayer for parents after they're gone. (That was especially true during that era—unlike today, when even many Orthodox synagogues allow women to say Kaddish, even if it is not technically required for them.)

According to Robert Crist, the historian who wrote an unpublished manuscript about her (*Mary Sachs: Merchant Princess*), the Sachses "coerced" Morris to attend *cheder*, an Orthodox school. Crist based this claim on two autobiographical "segments" Mary herself wrote (but never pulled together into a book). In Mary's view, the longing to have a "little kadishel" ended tragically, because her brother, "the sacrifice of an unenlightened point of view," was "unable to deal" with their father's death or with life in general.

Later Morris worked for Mary on her delivery trucks and like her, never married.

In 1920 Mary purchased the property at 208 North Third Street, the former home of Judge John H. Weiss, to open her first store. With cooperation from the Lowengard family, who still owned the building at 210 North Third, she was able to add a shoe store and beauty shop as well as lingerie, cosmetic, and jewelry departments.

A Lancaster store followed.

Beginning in 1925, Mary traveled at least once a year to Europe with one of her sisters, Hannah or Yetta, to observe the latest trends in fashion. She also made weekly trips to New York to visit clothing manufacturers. Her decision not to deal with Harrisburg salesmen assured her customers that their dresses would always be unique.

On the night of February 12, 1931, a fire started in the Harrisburg store's beauty shop. The building was nearly a total loss, and Mary had little insurance. The blaze caused $300,000 in damage, injured 12 firefighters, and left 13 apartment dwellers in the building homeless. Yet, she overcame several financial hurdles to rebuild her store. She hired local architects Lawrie and Green to design the new façade. And after seeing the work of interior architect Eleanor Le Maire on New York's Fifth Avenue, Mary Sachs hired her to design the inside.

After the fire that destroyed her original store, Mary drew on her life insurance to pay for the construction of the new building. But, according to columnist Mary Bradley in *The Patriot-News*, she built a $250,000 store, although she had collected only $53,000 in insurance.

On March 26, 1932, the new building opened. It had 21 departments. Six years later two additional floors were added, which made room for a nursery, children's shoe shop, slipper shop, two Trousseaux rooms, a fitting and alteration room, and a shop for nurse and maid uniforms. There were over a dozen consulting rooms.

Several thousand Harrisburgers attended the opening of the new renovated Mary Sachs shop on Saturday afternoon and evening. The building was the culmination of seven years of planning, which began two days after the fire.

The new building was thoroughly fireproofed and air conditioned throughout.

The first building, opened at 210 North Third Street in September 1918, was only a small part of the new building.

Hundreds of floral pieces and even more telegrams were sent to Mary on the occasion of her opening, and more than forty guests came from out-of-town for the affair. An open house was held Saturday afternoon and evening—with an informal tea in the afternoon followed that evening by a formal reception.

About 20 mannequins from New York, including three professional child models, displayed spring and early-summer fashions in the afternoon and evening. Refreshments were served on both occasions.

The ground and mezzanine floors of the new building were erected shortly after the fire; the two upper stories were added later.

By the 1950s Mary's shop had a doorman and valet parking. By 1954 the Harrisburg and Lancaster stores employed a total of 175 employees, and the Harrisburg store boasted a home goods section, paper shop, and candy shop. A few doors down, Mary Sachs also operated the 212 Men's Shop, a clothing store previously owned by Allen Stuart.

The business would eventually span the entire block of North Third Street between the old Harrisburger Hotel (now the Fulton Bank Building) and Cranberry Street, with several divisions.

Mary Sachs died on June 24, 1960. She was 72. The following day, the Mary Sachs Shop and the 212 Men's Shop closed in observance of her death. An advertisement read, "It is with profound sorrow that we make known the passing of Our Beloved Founder Mary Sachs."

Mary's sister Hannah Sachs Cantor became president of the Mary Sachs Shop and the 212 Men's Shop. Her sister Yetta Sachs Carpenter served as Secretary/Treasurer and continued to manage the Lancaster store, which had been under her care since 1927. The Reading shop, which was not managed by a Sachs family member, had closed in 1942.

The Harrisburg store celebrated its 50th Anniversary in 1968. Weeks later, the business was sold to Hess's Department Store, a chain based in Allentown. Hess's operated the store until its closing on September 2, 1978.

Mary Sachs was known for her philanthropy as well as for her innovative business practices. Throughout her lifetime she sought new ways to contribute to the community that was the cornerstone of her success. After meeting her at several charity events, Eleanor Roosevelt found in Mary Sachs "a philosophy that filled me with admiration."

The friendship between Mary and universally admired former First Lady went beyond the store and Mary's philanthropy. In a letter dated April 15, 1960, only a few months before Mary's passing, she wrote to Mrs. Roosevelt, expressing the hope that the former First Lady had "fully recovered from your recent accident." In fact, she called Mrs. Roosevelt "the First Lady of the Universe."

Before holding a press conference and addressing the United Jewish Appeal dinner at the JCC, Eleanor Roosevelt met for coffee and conversation in Mary's house. According to the *Patriot-News*, after Mrs. Roosevelt's trip to Harrisburg shortly before that exchange, the former First Lady sent Mary a photograph and, in Mary's words, "a lovely note" she would always "treasure" with a meaningful compliment. "That can only happen in this blessed land, that a mere struggling person like myself should be able to have the privilege and honor of not only listening to you, but sharing the dais with you, and that altogether short visit in my home has made my home a more complete home to live in."

The letter reflects Mary's florid writing style as well as her genuine appreciation for the country that had become her home.

In 1960, the Jewish community honored Mary Sachs by naming the main auditorium of the Jewish Community

Center in uptown Harrisburg after her, calling her a "great lady, humanitarian, and philanthropist." She was also referred to as the "Princess of Philanthropy," the flip side of the title by which she had already been known, 'The Merchant Princess."

Mary died a month later.

Historical Background

In one way, Mary Sachs was not unusual. According to the Jewish Women Encyclopedia of the Jewish Women's Archive, forty-four percent of the Jewish immigrants to the United States from 1886 to 1914 were women.

More than two million Jews from the Russian Empire, Romania, and Austria-Hungary who entered the United States in the years 1881 to 1924—when the American government imposed a restrictive quota system—came to stay.

Although some Jews had been peasants in Europe, many had not, but rather had lived in urban environments. Women often sold in the marketplace or were artisans, working along with men.

In those traditional families where husbands devoted themselves to studying Torah, women bore the major responsibility of breadwinning for their families.

Yet when they arrived in this country, like Mary's father, many became peddlers. It was also not uncommon for immigration to the New World to disrupt families, as it did in Mary's case. Married men often paved the way by immigrating first and then planning economically and in other ways for their wives and children, who came later.

In Mary's case, the family followed four years after her father had left for the United States, but often the period stretched into many years. Even with her husband working for a while in the States before she and the children came, Mary's mother still had to sell many of her belongings to afford passage.

Many Jewish immigrants worked in the burgeoning garment industry. Sometimes women worked at home or helped their husbands in mom-and-pop stores located close to home.

But according to the Jewish Women's Encyclopedia, still others became entrepreneurs to help the family income, such as pushcart peddlers. There is no indication that Mary's mother did any of these things, but they did have a large family.

Many women from the immigrant generation achieved high national, even international status. Think Helena Rubinstein and Estee Lauder (the latter had one Jewish parent) in the cosmetics industry and Ruth Handler and Beatrice Alexander in the doll business. Handler was the creator of the Barbie Doll and co-founder of the Mattel Company.

In the hospitality field, who doesn't know the name of Jennie Grossinger?

Mary Sachs might be said to be in the long line of Jewish women who combined an entrepreneurial and philanthropic spirit.

Beatrice Alexander, in particular, shared much in common with Mary Sachs. Also born into a world in which many women worked but few achieved prominence in business, Alexander grew up in the immigrant world (although, in New York City) and never lost sight of those less fortunate. She donated substantial sums to Jewish and non-Jewish causes alike, and was a committed Zionist. The words "pioneering businesswoman and a generous philanthropist" which applied to Alexander would apply to Mary Sachs as well.

Going further back in history was Dona Gracia Nasi, the adopted name for one of the most outstanding and richest women entrepreneurs. Although the vast majority of Jewish women were engaged in simple businesses, either in the marketplace or on its fringes, there were always the few who were rich and accomplished. The most outstanding of the women entrepreneurs, and the richest, was sixteenth-century Dona Gracia Nasi. After being widowed in 1935, she became heir to her husband's fortune, from gems and spices, and later was involved in banking.

Gracia Nasi spent much of her fortune on philanthropic works for the Jews, including the funding of the first Spanish-language version of the Hebrew Bible, the founding of a Jewish settlement in Tiberias (Palestine) and the rescue of secret Jews who were threatened by the Inquisition.

Glückel of Hameln left behind a memoir in Yiddish—one of the few extant writings by a woman of the period—that provides us with a picture both of seventeenth-century German-Jewish society and of the inner world of a woman of her place and time.

According to the Jewish Women's Archive, "Glückel was also an active partner in her husband's business, which consisted mainly of trading in jewelry and precious stones and, to a lesser degree, money-lending and financial transactions. Not only was she frequently asked for her advice and opinion, but she herself interviewed agents, considered potential business partners, etc. In addition she had 14 children, of which 12 survived.

On these shores, Abigail Minis of Savannah, Georgia, became a widow with eight children to support. She ran a family farm and retail business on her own.

Another American-Jewish phenomenon is the linking of the history of the American department store with the history of America's Jews, many with German roots. Among these were Abraham & Strauss, Neiman Marcus, I. Magnin, Gimbel's, Hochschild Kohn, Hecht's, Bloomingdale's, Filene's, and Bergdorf Goodman.

One leader in the department-store movement was Carrie Marcus Neiman, co-founder of the Neiman Marcus department store and an innovator in the department-store industry during the early-to-mid twentieth century. Marcus Neiman drew inspiration from European fashion and brought high-quality and cutting-edge merchandise to the Neiman Marcus stores and customers.

While analysts of this period speak of the conflict between being a woman, wife, and mother and an entrepreneur, this is one dilemma Mary avoided, perhaps deliberately, by not marrying. Yet, the sisters in business with her, Hannah and Yetta, did marry.

According to the late Prof. Paula Hyman, married Jewish women worked outside the home in much smaller numbers than did other immigrant women, because immigrant Jewish men were highly skilled and usually endowed with entrepreneurial talent relative to other immigrants. Jewish men often shared the common cultural norm that if a wife worked outside the home, it reflected on the husband's failure to support his family. This, again, was not a consideration for a single woman like Mary.

Yet married or unmarried, according to Hyman, Jewish immigrant women who worked felt freer; that is certainly a sentiment Mary would have understood.

Hyman further noted that with upward mobility and increasing leisure time, immigrant women and their daughters often joined such Jewish women's organizations as Hadassah and the National Council of Jewish Women, "which built on a triple legacy: traditional Jewish philanthropy, the nineteenth-century Ladies Aid Society, and the U.S. Women's Club movement." This too Mary could relate to; she was an early pioneer of sorts in becoming involved in organizations, such as the United Jewish Community, where men predominated till later.

In Leon Harris's book *Merchant Princes: An Intimate History of Jewish Families Who Built Great Department Stores*, the author discusses the role of women in the management of some of the country's great department stores. While again, Mary was on her own, the strength exhibited by other Jewish women who operated "behind the scenes" was found in her.

Another Jewish-founded and owned enterprise was that of Nan Duskin, the internationally known boutique that dressed the best of Philadelphia's high society for nearly 70 years, beginning in 1927.

According to Andrew R. Heinze, a former professor of American history, Jewish women played a disproportionate role in the development of American consumer culture because of a combination of factors. "For one, American industry became increasingly consumer-oriented, and consumer industries were comparatively open to small entrepreneurs. For another, Jewish immigrants and their children tended to display strong entrepreneurial tendencies," moving onto commercial pursuits ranging from clothing to furniture to real estate to movies.

Estelle Sommers, the founder of the Capezio brand of dance wear, and designer Anne Klein were among the other entrepreneurial Jewish women of the last century. Not to mention Diane Von Furstenberg and Donna Karan.

There are many more.

Whether her name is known to them or not, all of these women stood on Mary's shoulders.

General background on Jewish women and their response to the American consumer economy is provided by Andrew R. Heinze, *Adapting to Abundance: Jewish Immigrants, Mass Consumption and the Search for American Identity* (1990); for a survey of the subject of Jewish women in business, see Irene D. Neu, "The Jewish Businesswoman in America," *American Jewish Historical Quarterly 66* (September 1976): 137-154; and Heinze, "Advertising and Consumer Culture in the United States." *Jewish Women: A Comprehensive Historical Encyclopedia.* 1 March 2009. *Jewish Women's Archive.* (Viewed on September 20, 2014)

The Origins

The difficult path from harsh childhood to the role of successful entrepreneur and community benefactor as an adult in Harrisburg, Pennsylvania, began for Mary Sachs in 1888 in Lithuania, then under the control of Russia. She was born on March 10 of that year, the third of three sisters at that time, to Jewish parents.

In autobiographical notes years later, Mary would look back at the difficulties of her childhood not too kindly.

She viewed her mother, Fannie, as too much of a disciplinarian. She recalled an incident when on a shopping trip in a Russian village she lingered to "gaze at something that attracted my attention," Mary wrote in her unfinished autobiographical notes. Maybe the pause reflected an early feel for shopping. Her mother had her spanked—by a "strong, healthy-looking individual," the shopkeeper of a men's hat shop.

That was after Fannie had tried, unsuccessfully, to yank her away by the arm.

Although she came to forgive her mother later on, Mary wrote that during her adolescent years she wondered "whether my mother—unfortunately—lost an opportunity to give this child a little tenderness, care, a little affection and love."

Yet, in that era of Eastern European life, it was not unusual for a father to emigrate first in search of a livelihood before sending for the rest of the family to join him. And a mother, taking care of their children by herself with limited economic resources (and often under stressful conditions) might be excused for applying excessive discipline. When Mary was four, her mother felt it was time to leave the village, too, although not sure exactly where her husband was located in America.

"My mother decided to convert her furs and the remaining part of her trousseau (into cash) so she could take her three little ones to the U.S.," Mary wrote. "Mother carried me to save half fare but kept complaining about the weight and burden."

Another version of that story had the mother also selling her hair to gain enough money for passage.

As stated above, Mary was a Russian-born immigrant who was only four years old when she came to America in 1892 with her mother, Fanny Rhoads Sachs, and two siblings, Sarah and Emma. The family found husband and father Wolf Sachs in Renovo, a town in the lumber and coal region of northern Pennsylvania. Wolf Sachs was a peddler and shop owner who had immigrated four years before the rest of his family. Around 1900, the Sachs family moved to Baltimore where Lena, Esther, Morris, Yetta, and Hannah were born.

The chronological order of the eight children was, as niece Rachel Katzen of Harrisburg recalls, Sarah, Emma, Mary, Lena, Morris, Yetta and Hannah.

After spending a short time in Baltimore, Mary Sachs moved to Steelton where she worked first in a candy shop and then in an installment store where she was promoted and eventually made manager. After several moves, the rest of the Sachs family joined her in the Harrisburg area around 1916.

Mary began developing her knack for the retail trade at Kaufman's Department Store on Harrisburg's Market Square. In 1910 she left Kaufman's for William Schleisner's, a highly respected women's clothing store where she worked for eight years.

In 1918 Mary Sachs was introduced to Harry Lowengard, who operated a printing shop on Third Street. He loaned her seed money and rented to her the first floor of his building so she could open her own clothing store.

Because of her small amount of capital, Mary carefully planned the layout of the store so that her limited stock was not kept on the floor. Instead, customers were seated in private booths and saleswomen presented them with individually selected garments. The store opened on September 6, 1918. With sales of over $200,000 in its first year, the shop quickly became one of Harrisburg's premier retail locations. Stores in Lancaster (1921) and Reading (1923) followed.

When you consider how soon after the opening of the Harrisburg store Mary opened the additional ones, her drive seems even more impressive. When you add to that the fact that she had little or no formal education and came to the United States not knowing the language, her accomplishments appear even more so.

Mary made frequent trips to Paris to attend the openings of the famous couturiers on the Rue de la Paix to make her stores an "instant mirror," according to Donehoo, of the mode expressed on that famous street.

Not all her trips were strictly about business. *The Harrisburg Telegraph* printed a photograph of Mary and her sisters Yetta and Hannah landing on the S. S. Majestic in New York City after a two-month stay in Europe. Mary, the clipping indicated, was a delegate to the second annual conference of the World Union for Progressive Judaism in London—representing Ohev Sholom Temple in Harrisburg. After some sightseeing the three sisters attended the fall openings in Paris.

In an interview Mary gave to *The Harrisburg Telegraph*, which appeared on February 27, 1926, she said: "Elaborate accessories to every costume, gorgeous in colors, suggestive of Spain, Egypt and the Orient, are the essentials for the well-dressed woman, according to the Paris mode."

The compliment was returned. After Paul Poiret, a leading French fashion designer during the first two decades of the 20th century, whose contributions to his field have been compared to Picasso's legacy, visited the three Mary Sachs stores in 1927, he wrote to Mary that they are "charming" and "completely Parisian." He continued: "I would not have credited that an American city the size of Harrisburg could present models of such artistry and sophistication . . . It is very clear that you maintain contact with my beloved Paris."

In 1953, when an ailing Mary accepted the chairmanship of an Israel Bond drive in Harrisburg that was to feature a concert by noted violinist Mischa Elman, she wrote a letter to the community expressing her gratitude that her parents had chosen the United States as their destination instead of some other country.

It also included this comment on the ocean voyage that brought her and her family to this country:

". . . It happened to be a ship, perhaps with a load of cargo, steerage only, that took five weeks of torturous seasickness . . . Believe me, I was four years old and I remember every bit of that seasickness and the want of food and medication, and the need of a bed for my poor mother . . . to lie in, instead of the (tiered) boarded cots."

Elsewhere in her papers, Mary also recalled the restraints on her childish instincts to roam about the decks.

"It was because of the hardships, there was always an estrangement between my mother and me," she wrote in a memoir.

Later in life, Mary would sort out the traumas of her early years and put them into a more positive perspective.

"I have never forgotten what it means to be given the privilege of freedom—freedom of thinking, freedom of expression, freedom of work; for I, as a child, had never been given time for the play world, the toy world, the make-believe world," she wrote in that 1953 letter. "It has always been the factual and the real. I pray to our Heaven that, if I had my life to live over again, I should not be denied that early experience, for I needed it so much to live by and to work by."

It appears that freedom remained a theme throughout Mary's life.

She added in her autobiographical notes, "It was that memory that makes it possible for me to work and try to keep well, to do more work, and in so doing I will be able to share with the less fortunate men, women, and children."

That drive to help others would dominate her life to its end.

Looking back years later, Mary took a more positive view of her mother and their relationship.

Shortly before her death, she told a Harrisburg audience through the pain of illness, "Mother was my inspiration. Early in life, I did not like her. Later in life, I learned to love her."

She did not speak on that occasion of her father.

Later, Hannah and Yetta expressed appreciation to their mother for teaching them the value of family unity, hard work, and a sense of personal responsibility "within the context of the Jewish faith." Mary referred to her mother's legacy in one written (but unpublished) memoir.

> "To my mother, I owe my first true conception of the real meaning of prayer," she commented. "She told me that prayer should never take the place of work and effort on my part. From this, I learned my first great lesson about prayer—that I was not to pray to God in Santa Claus fashion, a way that is cheapening and degrading a conception of God."

Though Mary (and Hannah, the youngest sibling, at least) had "negative" impressions of their father, Mary still bought a house for her parents when they moved to Harrisburg on Green Street.

To prove that she also could record some less anguished girlish memoirs, Mary once wrote of those early days in Renovo, Pa., where the family had been reunited:

"When a little girl, my pride and joy was my hair. It was thick and bushy and I would wear it open so that the wind would blow through it. So everyone would stop and remark about the beautiful child and her gorgeous hair."

The family eventually moved to Baltimore when the lumber boom had faded in Pennsylvania, Crist's monograph added.

Mary's pre-Mary Sachs Store career was rocky.

She went to work in a cigar factory but was dismissed, Hannah recalled, "because she took Saturday afternoons off to the theater." But not before she had become self-supporting.

Eventually, Mary moved to Steelton, where she worked in a short-lived candy store, then in a store selling goods on the installment plan, where she was promoted and eventually made manager. Wolf resumed work, owning a dry good store, then another, and riding circuit with goods piled in a wagon.

After several moves, the rest of the Sachs family joined her in the Harrisburg area around 1916.

According to Michael Coleman's *The Jews of Harrisburg: An Informal History by a Native Son*, Mary lived in Steelton with one of her sisters, Sarah, earning $6 a week and commuting to Harrisburg to work.

In Harrisburg she worked for Kaufman's Department Store on Market Square, where co-workers, she felt, treated her with disdain.

In 1910, Mary went to work at Schleisner's, a woman's clothing store, at the recommendation of a friend. Schleisner recognized some good qualities in her and promoted her. Eventually, she became an assistant buyer and even would babysit for the owners' son.

"When he became ill," according to Hannah's oral history, "Mr. Schleisner wrote into his will that Mary should have a job for life. But a visiting manufacturer overheard her telling a customer that the item he was interested in was going on sale the next day and he should wait to buy it. Mrs. Schleisner had her locked out of the store."

Another story about Mary, of almost mythic proportions, is the time when as a stock girl, she was helping to sell scarves and fur coats by the store's door. Because of the freezing temperatures, no other sales person wanted to take the post by the door. But Mary did. That might be considered a metaphor for her being willing to go out in the cold and form her own business.

A customer asked her about the quality of the merchandise at the store. Her reply:

> "Do you know the man who owns this business? He's a good man, a man with principles and integrity. He is a respected member of the community. A man's business and the product he sells should always take on the character of the man himself."

The customer was convinced, according to Coleman, paid his money and left with his purchase. He also spread the story and later returned to buy a fur coat from Mary for his daughter. Also impressed was the store owner, who promoted her.

Mary had learned well along the way, and, by the time of losing her position at Schleisners had some idea about how a store should be run. Having no job, she decided to act on suggestions that she go into business on her own.

With a little money but a lot of dreams, she readied herself to tackle the commercial marketplace on her own terms in 1918, an era when it was unusual for a woman to go out on her own in the business world.

She managed to raise enough money to begin operations.

In his extensive 1925 history of Harrisburg and Dauphin County, George P. Donehoo included a section on Mary Sachs and her shop.

> "Completely unspoiled by her success, she impresses one as being decidedly surprised and not a little startled at finding

herself at the head of a powerful commercial enterprise," he wrote. "Others, however, affirm that her success is but the inevitable expression of exceptional ability coupled with a sterling character."

Donehoo spoke of the "unique methods" the Mary Sachs Store achieved, also calling it an "example of the flowering of exceptional commercial talent under the fostering influence of a favorable environment."

Thanks to the difficulties Mary encountered working for others, the Harrisburg area community was to gain a legendary retail operation—whose reputation would spread beyond the region's borders. The community also was to gain a pillar of charitable support that would outlast both the person and the enterprise she founded.

In his Harrisburg and Dauphin County history, George P. Donehoo wrote that Mary's plan of displaying frocks "only in the actual fitting booths was novel. Her advertising which never named price nor described an article of merchandise was thought impracticable, and a waste of space."

In 1925, the year Donehoo's history came out, the combined volume of the three stores totaled $600,000—only seven years after the first had opened.

THE STORES

On September 6, 1918, Mary opened her first store, in downtown Harrisburg.

That first year, the business did a volume of more than $200,000.

Mary Sachs brought to her new venture some experience, very little capital, a willingness to innovate, and some ideas about the kind of merchandising she wanted to do, ideas that eventually became a widely discussed philosophy of business as she garnered success.

Leon and Harry Lowengard, who ran the *Courier Press*, a newspaper that focused on the Jewish community, or at least one of them, was willing to take a chance and rent space to this then 30-year-old woman at their 210 North Third Street building in Harrisburg.

She had been working at low retail wages so had no big nest egg to tap into; moreover, her family was closer to poverty than to affluence. But she managed to scrape up, through loans and a line of credit arranged by a businessman, some $6000, according to Donohoo, in his 1925 history. It would be a modest shop at first, some 20 feet by 106 feet.

While she had learned where and what to buy in her New York marketplace, not all manufacturers would sell to her. Perhaps it was the uncertainty of dealing with a young woman entrepreneur in an era when women simply did not take on such a role.

Not wanting to offend existing customers in the area, including those of the Schleisner store, surely was part of that resistance she met.

In any event, Mary finessed that problem.

When the store opened on September 6, 1918, younger sister Hannah recalled in an oral history tape at the State Archives, Mary "brought $100 worth of flowers, putting cards of congratulations she signed herself with the names of manufacturers, even those who wouldn't sell her any clothes. Mrs. Schleisner sent an employee to check out the opening. When that employee reported the bouquets and notes, Schleisner canceled her orders. Those manufacturers, stuck with the merchandise, then called Mary to see if they would ship it to her."

The flowers, writers about the store later would report, intrigued at least one manufacturer who came to see for himself. Regretting that he had not really sent a bouquet himself, he decided to sell Mary merchandise.

According to Elaine Hermann, writing in *Central Penn Business Journal* in February 1990, he "promised on the spot to supply her store with his designs. . . . Such cunning acts, along with a sleepless philanthropic spirit, have made the name of Mary Sachs a bright memory in the minds of many of the region's business people and charitable organizations."

Still, there was a limit to how much Mary could buy with her available funds. So she instituted a practice that, though mothered by necessity, became a landmark of her retail operation. To prevent customers from not seeing crowded racks of clothing, she had a series of private booths set up and staff would hand-carry garments to the waiting customer.

Larger urban stores would pick up that concept.

"Throughout the 1920s, [Mary's] retailing concept was copied by shops in major east coast cities . . . Sachs extended that personal service in every way possible," Hermann also wrote in a 1990 *Central Pennsylvania Business Journal* article recalling the elegance of the shops. "Clothes would be brought for selection to the homes of the housebound."

In the era during which Mary opened her shop, there was no shortage of local competition for the woman shopper's business.

By 1920, a tribute to Mary Sachs's financial and advertising success in a history of The Wednesday Club—a Harrisburg cultural group—noted that there were 10 stores selling women's clothing and 73 dressmakers offering their services.

"If the carriage trade was to be weaned from the 73 who provided custom-made dresses, it would need a store that gave equally personal attention to each customer," that writer observed.

In dollar terms, Mary's strategy did well. As stated earlier, Donehoo's 1925 history records that the Sachs shops—by then there was also one in Lancaster, which opened in 1921, and one in Reading, which opened in 1924 and closed in 1945—were grossing more than $600,000 a year.

By 1954, when Sam Feinberg of *Women's Wear Daily*, a national trade journal, wrote a six-part series about the Mary Sachs operation, the Harrisburg and Lancaster stores were reportedly doing more than $2 million worth of business annually.

Success could be measured in more than dollars alone, however. There was the success of Mary's merchandising philosophy and acceptance by the Central Pennsylvania consumers.

That was not always ensured.

Historian Donehoo recorded some of the negativism of that early period:

"Never before had the women of this city seen displayed outside New York apparel of such complete sophistication. People shook their heads and predicted disaster. 'A provincial public would never buy such completely modish models,' (the thinking went). 'She was shooting over the heads of Harrisburg."

Mary's aim, though, proved remarkably accurate.

Her charitable inclinations also were appreciated.

As Hermann wrote in her 1990 *Central Pennsylvania Business Journal* article "At the same time that her shop was acquiring its reputation for quality and personal service, Sachs's philanthropic deeds were earning her the gratitude and respect of the community."

Details of that phase of Mary's communal life will follow later.

What was the Sachs philosophy of retailing?

One college press release, announcing a scholarship fund established in Sachs's name, commented that her "interest was in presenting not stylish clothes but simple, basic, beautiful clothes, clothes which derive their charm from good lines and exquisite workmanship."

Women's Wear Daily columnist Feinberg declared that the shop . . . expresses "fashion, not style. As Miss Sachs explains this policy, 'In style you no sooner buy it then it is out of date; fashion is updated. We don't go in for a lot of the novelties, even though we know we lose sales that way."

As sister Hannah once summed it up: It was "fashion, not fad." She was in the position to know, having quit school at 15 to work in Mary's still-new (at the time) store as a delivery girl—by foot and by streetcar. Eventually she succeeded to the presidency of the operation after Mary's death.

Yvonne Milspaw, in a 1998 *Central PA* Magazine reminiscence about the Mary Sachs experience, observed, "Mary Sachs interviewed each customer at length, recommending not only quality and styles she thought would most suit their clothing needs and social lives, but sometimes also introducing changes that had to be handled delicately— new foundation garments or even a new hairstyle. She did it with such warmth charm and authority . . . that instead of hurt feelings, her suggestions were met with thanks or praise."

Hannah and sister Yetta, who managed the Lancaster store, would alternate yearly trips with Mary to Paris, where they observed the designer fashion shows and life in general. One year, Yetta told Mary she thought the undergarment prices in Paris were excessive.

Mary replied, "Unless a woman is well-dressed underneath, no matter what you sell her or what she wears, she's not properly dressed."

Another Sachs quote: "If you can't wear a coat four or five years, it was the wrong coat the day you bought it. Likewise with a suit; likewise with a dress."

Explaining her new store in that city, Mary expounded for a Lancaster newspaper the policy that built her business in Harrisburg as being "not how much we can get for what we give but how much we can give for what we get."

Bob Crist's monograph explained another philosophy, one Mary expressed in 1938: "I will continue, as always, to be an architect of a complete ensemble—a builder of the finished costume, not a mere medium through which a single garment can be purchased."

Crist also noted that she was careful not to embarrass customers by selling acquaintances identical clothing; this was a tactic not unique to her but characteristic of her. "Her disdain of faddishness showed through in some of her harsh criticisms of passing styles, like the chemise dress and trapeze dress," he wrote.

"No word in the English language can dignify the gunny sack now being foisted on the American woman," Mary said of the sack dress, for example. "I am aware . . . that this store must be guided by its patrons . . . Neither is it a mental institution . . . I don't think that we have a moral right to sponsor fashions that make a woman look ridiculous."

As one Mary Sachs ad about short skirts concluded, "Don't be swayed by up-to-the-minute if it isn't up to your standards."

Feinberg's series of articles observes that gift-wrapping for special occasions was emphasized by the store.

"A loss is sustained on the minimum charge for these packages," he wrote, "but that service has proved one of the firm's leading 'messengers for prestige.' Sales are held only twice a year [more frequently later] in order to protect regular customers. Garments, which are moving, are not reduced in price. Nothing is bought for the sales . . . Two or three times a year, the store runs a 'refurbishing' ad. The public is invited to bring in clothes, regardless of where purchased, to have them repaired and generally freshened up. It is all performed in the store's own workroom. Again, it is done at a loss but Miss Sachs describes the service as a 'wonderful feature because it has made many customers for us.'"

Mary had a very honest reputation as a saleswoman. Hannah would recall, "When somebody wanted to buy something and she didn't think it would be right, she told him (or her)."

Untraditional advertising, by the way, was another hallmark of this retailer's presentation to the public. It featured no merchandise or prices, just Mary's thoughts about a wide range of subjects that interested her, be they fashion trends or holiday celebrations, history or social changes, customer correspondence, or thanks to employees, among others. In effect, they were mini-editorials, eye-catching in format and thought-provoking in content.

Naturally, columnists found them noteworthy.

"I first began suspecting the bigheartedness of Miss Sachs when, years ago, I began reading her advertising," wrote *Women's Wear Daily* columnist Kenneth Collins in 1960. "It is a campaign that has no exact parallel. Week after week, Miss Sachs discusses . . . anything that appeals to her generous, acute and stimulating mind. Reading these ads is a revealing experience."

Historian Donehoo wrote, "Her advertising was thought impractical and a waste of time." But, he added, "These methods brought quick successes."

Hannah recalled in her oral history tape that Mary initially used a Chicago ad agency and that the approach she settled on was dictated by necessity.

"She didn't have a lot of financial help," Hannah reminisced. "She had to promote her fashions through her point of view and through a story about them. She didn't show a picture of her fashions because she couldn't afford to pay an artist's fee. Then, after a while, she was told about a man in New York, Frank Irving Fletcher. This man created copy in an institutional fashion."

Fletcher would write the Mary Sachs ads for two decades.

"When Mary would go to New York, she'd visit Fletcher and tell him things that happened to her and interested her," Hannah added. "He would develop the ads."

Commonwealth Magazine commented in 1949 that Mary Sachs's advertising features "her deep feelings for the community in which she operates."

One interesting example of the Sachs-Fletcher approach was an ad that featured a letter to the store from a mother of three boys who had expressed appreciation about the case of shopping for her sons in the store. A picture of the three boys at the top of the ad was accompanied at the bottom by an open letter to the youngsters signed by Mary Sachs:

"Dear Ronald, Donald and Thomas:

There are two ways in which a boy can get his picture in the paper. First by being good. Second by being no good! The first is chiefly dependent on the influence of the parents. The second is chiefly dependent on you. Parents can't do everything. They can cherish and guide you till you are old enough to face the world alone. After that, it's up to you to lead decent and useful lives. Never fail those who have never failed you. Live up to the lessons you learned at home, and may you live long and happily in the years to come."

The middle section of the ad included Mary's appreciation for the mother's compliment, reading, "I am well rewarded for anything I have done to deserve a mother's praise."

As an editorial writer for *The Patriot-News* in Harrisburg, Bern Sharfman, author of the original version of this monograph about Mary and her sisters (published by the Mary Sachs Trust in 2003), said that he especially enjoyed the ads that editorialized on what was happening in town. Long before the newspaper took official notice of it, for example, Sharfman wrote, Mary was belaboring the Pennsylvania Railroad for the deterioration in service she experienced during her weekly New York trips.

Women's Wear Daily columnist Kenneth Collins called reading Mary's ads a "revealing experience." Other topics Mary explored in them were nurses; the way to assist the drive to cure arthritis; National Secretaries Week; the excellence of America's fashion magazines; and the obligations of a store to its employees.

"When is a nickel a nuisance?" Mary Sachs "editorialized" another time as the use of parking meters spread. "A nickel is a nuisance when you have to dash out of the Mary Sachs shop to put another nickel in the parking meter . . . Your peace of mind is no longer dependent on a parking meter's appetite for nickels. When you drive up to the Mary Sachs store, a uniformed attendant takes charge of your car. When you leave, notify him a few minutes in advance and he will bring your car around again."

Jerry Fried, a Harrisburger who was a national guru on retail furniture sales, often would say that the goal of advertising was not so much to sell a specific item, but when a customer needed your type of merchandise, to have your store high on his or her list of shops to visit for it. Mary's advertising certainly helped achieve that.

These touches added up to a formula for success, making a Mary Sachs shopping trip a fruitful and interesting experience for customers.

Through the years, what Mary called her "Congress of Unusual Shops" grew in size.

Donehoo noted, "The Harrisburg shop has been enlarged to several times its original dimensions and now embraces, in addition to its apparel departments, a shoe shop, beauty salon, a Treasure Box for sale of perfumery, novelties, jewelry, boudoir accessories, etc."

Bob Crist's monograph adds to that picture by observing, "The beauty shop also provided the services of a chiropodist and high 'colonic' treatments and sauna baths, supervised by the chiropodist's sister, a Registered Nurse."

Hannah, in her oral history, summed it up by saying Mary "eventually broke through a wall on the Lowengard property and got more space to open various departments."

Both WWD columnist Feinberg in his series about the shops and Yvonne Milspaw in her *Central PA* magazine article mentioned the purchase of a private dwelling adjoining the original store as an impetus for expansion.

"(She) turned each room into an individual boutique and added a restaurant for her employees in the basement," Milspaw wrote.

Mary's clothing also had her own label in them.

What kind of boss was he? Mary is, Feinberg wrote, a "benevolent despot" to her employees but "wants to know about illness and takes care of financial assistance confidentially. She serves a hot lunch to employees at a nominal cost and provides a free dinner if they work at night."

Mary also could be a painstaking taskmaster, according to Feinberg. Once, he saw her stop and correct a salesgirl who was dragging a dress across the floor. He heard Mary tell her: "Merchandise should be fondled—carried as if it were a baby; this creates a wonderful impression in the customer's mind."

The Feinberg article added, "Similarly she noticed some dust on a showcase and mentioned it to a buyer. Miss Sachs said she always remembered something Bishop Brown, former dean of the School of Retailing at the University of Pittsburgh, once told her: 'The first thing he taught students was to keep a cloth handy because their department and stock had to be spotless.'"

Mary's path to success from the 1918 opening of her first store was not smooth or untroubled, however.

As mentioned earlier, dramatic adversity came in the form of fire in February 1931. Two months earlier, on New Year's Eve, Mary had an open house there in honor of the marriage of Hannah to Benjamin Cantor, who operated a shoe store a few blocks away. Mary had an apartment set up in the store's building for the Cantors, too.

"A watchman came and knocked at our door to tell us the place was on fire," Hannah recalled in her oral history tape. "Capitol Park was like a circus, filled with people. It was cold. Some wonderful customers came down to offer their homes to us."

Rabbi Philip David Bookstaber, a force in Mary's life not only as a rabbi but also as a close friend, told Mary, who was in New York, to go to the theater that night as she had planned and come back to Harrisburg the next day. The two had met in 1924 and had been friends since.

"When Mary got off the train, the press was there to meet her. And they asked, 'What are your plans?' 'We're going to build a bigger and better place' (she replied). "We weren't insured for the full amount," Hannah added.

Mary pushed ahead with her plans.

"Rabbi Bookstaber took money from his insurance to help finance the opening," Hannah continued. A week later, "the (Lancaster) bank where she deposited the money folded in the Depression. When Mary told the Rabbi, he said, 'I didn't loan the money to the bank. I loaned it to Mary Sachs. I'll get it back with interest.' He did."

Indeed, among the family papers are canceled checks to Rabbi Bookstaber, one in the 1940s marked "payment in full."

"After the fire, we moved to the old Harrisburger Hotel," Hannah said. "Mary went to get ideas for her new store in Manhattan. She saw one not yet ready to open on 57th Street and liked the way it looked. She was told it had been designed by Eleanor Le Maire."

She contacted Le Maire, who agreed to come to Harrisburg to design the new store. Harrisburg architects Lawrie & Green did the work. As Bob Crist explains in his monograph, they created a "two-story façade" that pulled everything together and gave the place a sense of unity it had lacked.

"The new store," Crist reports, "offered 21 departments. The store reopened in March of 1932. In 1937, two more floors and a higher façade were added for more expansion, including a nursery, little lady shop, slippers and maids and nurses uniforms.

The Mary Sachs stores were open 6 days a week, and all the stores were open Thursday night till 9 or 9:30.

Perhaps the innovation most associated with Mary Sachs was the absence of racks. The salespeople would bring a customer clothing, saying you look good in this or that. If alterations were needed, they'd call a tailor—there were three or four on the premises.

The fashions were Paris styles.

Another change came in 1946 when, Crist records, "Clothier Allen Stuart is persuaded to link his men's shop to Mary's store, creating the 212 Men's Shop."

Stuart eventually opened his own independent store again, but the 212 Men's Shop continued as part of the Mary Sachs operation.

The Lancaster store also grew.

When Yetta went to work there shortly after it opened, Crist wrote, it was located at 138-40 North King Street, and "had 45 by 85 feet of selling space. At first, Yetta commuted by train daily from Harrisburg to Lancaster. Eventually she moved to Lancaster.

Based on a variety of accounts, Mary Sachs persevered and, with the help of friends, family, and her own assets, managed to come back bigger and better than ever after that 1931 tragedy. One often-repeated story is that after a credit agency turned her down after the fire, one member of the rating committee, who had been impressed by her presentation, offered Mary a personal loan to help out.

Shortly afterwards, Mary bought a home at 2917 North Front Street in Harrisburg—where Le Maire used her designing talents too. Hannah and her husband, Ben, accepted an invitation to move in, bringing with them a Steinway grand piano from Troup's Music Store on Market Square as a house gift.

Le Maire's work on both the store and house, which came to be known as "Castle Mary Sachs," would be featured in pictorial displays in the March 1936 issue of *The Architectural Record*, a national publication.

Mary died on June 24, 1960, at age 72 in Memorial Hospital in New York City, where she had undergone an operation for cancer. Hannah became president of the stores; Yetta continued to manage the Lancaster shop and served as secretary-treasurer. Edythe Gross, who handled more than the financial details of the business, stayed on. She had become known to many customers as Mary's alter ego—imposing the boss's philosophy of merchandising and treating customers, including smoothing of any ruffled feathers.

Mary would pay tribute to others for contributing to the store's success. She told Sam Feinberg during his Harrisburg visit she was grateful to manufacturers from whom she bought items for teaching her "what to do and what not to do."

In one of her patented ads one New Year's holiday, Mary expanded on that theme:

"This New Year's brings home to me once again how indebted I am to my customers, to my resources, and to my employees for ideas . . . I have known it for 30 years. I have known that this business at every step of its development is an echo of voluntary suggestions of others. Even my own ideas are mostly unconscious interpretations of all that I hear in the course of a day's work."

No doubt there is a gem of truth in that statement, but one also detects a forced note of modesty. The philosophy Mary espoused, chronicled in this chapter, reveals a highly personal, hands-on approach for retailing for which she merited the accolades others would give her.

That same ad also revealed her thinking about expansion.

"Someone wondered why I don't open a flock of Mary Sachs stores in different cities and get in step with the trend of a Chain Store Age. The reasons are simple. I am too individual in my approach to fashion to be a link in a chain. And the women I cater to are too individual in their requirements to be counseled by proxy. They want the intimate, personal attention of one store and not the divided devotion of a scattered audience. I have a fierce attachment to Harrisburg . . . It's my town, and I love it . . . Nothing could ever induce me to make a whistle stop of the great State Capital of Pennsylvania."

Of course, Mary had two stores, not one, and had tried a third in Reading, which she eventually had to close down. Stung once by the difficulty of extending her philosophy outward, she may have shied away from it. It is true, though, that she disliked the mass marketing of the larger, more impersonal stores that were then spreading across the country.

In 1968, eight years after Hannah took rein of the shops—and a few weeks after the actual date of the business's 50th anniversary, she announced the sale of Mary Sachs to Hess's Department Store, based in Allentown, Pa. It was a decision she said later she regretted.

So a business that had prospered despite adversity, that had brought national attention to Harrisburg, that had employed about 200 people at its peak—including several relatives—that had fueled Mary's charitable instincts and had attracted a loyal clientele of leading area families like the Baileys and McCormicks, and some national celebrities, was about to enter its final stage.

This coincided with the decline if not demise of downtown Harrisburg, a trend the city is now trying to reverse.

One of Mary's prominent customers, former First Lady Mamie Eisenhower, dictated this note to her personal secretary, who forwarded it to Hannah, from a sick bed in Walter Reed Hospital:

"I noticed in the *Women's Wear Daily* that Mary Sachs has been sold to a company by the name of Hess and that you will no longer be with the shop. I am distressed to learn this, for I always looked forward to making my selections through you. I realize you wanted to retire, but we shall miss you very much. Dr. Milton Eisenhower was here last week with his daughter, Ruth, and we talked of the many years that the Eisenhowers have done their shopping at Mary Sachs."

Crist's monograph includes this anecdote. "President Eisenhower, visiting Harrisburg for the William Penn Museum's (now State Museum) Wyeth Art Show, stopped at the store to buy things for his wife. When thanked for his visit, he told Hannah, 'Mamie would have killed me if I hadn't stopped.'"

In 1945, when news of President Franklin D. Roosevelt's death came, *Patriot-News* columnist Paul Beers recalled in a 1982 column, "Mary Sachs, a close friend of Mrs. Roosevelt, immediately closed the store."

Beers also referred to Mary, five years after her death, "as a romantic at heart, but a realist in emergencies."

An admirer, Beers called Mary "as incisive a mind, as energetic a vision, and as warm a heart as this town has known." (March 1982)

Further, according to Beers's March 1982 column, years ago, in a friendly debate at the United Way, a gentleman remarked that Mary might be getting "too emotional" about an issue. "Her eyes glared," Beers wrote. 'As soon as my emotions stop functioning,' she said. 'I will no longer be here.' He commented that even several years after her death, "her emotions haven't stopped functioning."

"This is a town at dinner parties, and nobody ever gave more elegant ones than Miss Sachs, a lady who was an unprepossessing 5-foot-2, sold the best line of clothing in town, but had no compulsion to doll herself up and was, in the matter of formal education, probably not a grammar-school graduate," he wrote further.

Whatever genius is, she had it, said Bruce E. Cooper, board chairman of Harrisburg Area Community College (in Beers's same column). "She liked to stay 30 years ahead of the times," Cooper said. "You know, I think her ideas are still 30 years ahead today."

All her charitable giving was done in the name of her employees.

Mary's mother, Fannie Sachs.

Mary's father, Wolf Sachs.

Harrisburg store, rebuilt and expanded after 1931 fire.

Robert Kleinman introduces Mary Sachs at the 1960
dinner at which the JCC auditorium was named for her.

Eleanor Roosevelt and Mary Sachs adjust their corsages at a fund-raising
dinner in Harrisburg.

Mary Sach's house in uptown Harrisburg.

A Wall of Honors at the Harrisburg store.

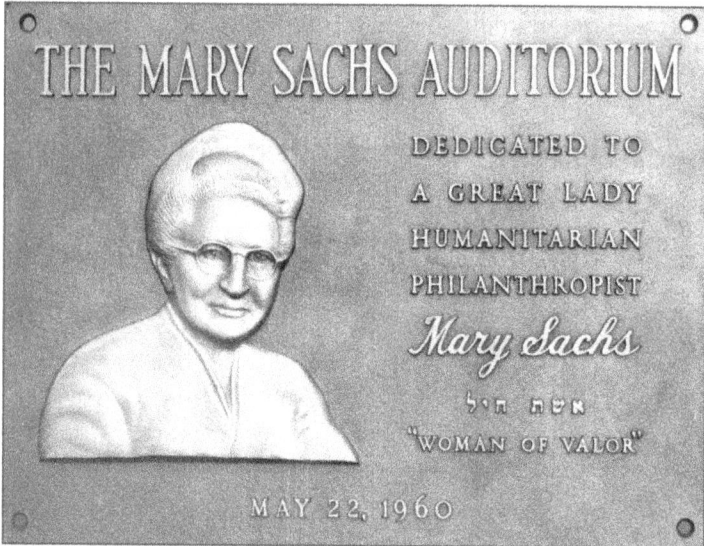

The plaque naming the Harrisburg JCC auditorium for Mary Sachs.

Mary's sisters Hannah and Yetta.

Harrisburg Telegraph special section about reopened
store in the capital city.

Interior of Harrisburg store.

urge you to visit this de-
you will settle your Christ-
g problems easily and
leasantly.

Mary Sachs

LANCASTER   HARRISBURG   READING

HARRISBURG

My dear Friends:

As you well know, Feb. 11, 1931, a wonderful
structure that had been a private residence
turned into a very unusual specialty shop,
met with the catastrophe of a fire which
completely destroyed the edifice. At that
time I suffered two tremendous losses---one,
of a home store building, and the other the
loss of time to render service to my public.

There was nothing to do but to plan a new
home immediately. Of course, since it would
not be possible to replace the old dwelling,
I decided to erect a building with the new
modern note that would truly render a service
to this community at a very low overhead.

We stand ready to serve every woman and miss
of discriminating taste who understands the
right kind of service rendered by my very
efficient staff, whom I am very proud to have
with me for many years---in fact, many of my
employees have been with me ever since this
business was started September 8, 1918.

I do hope you will find every comfort in this
new establishment, for that was my intention
in the planning of this very beautiful new
home.

Sincerely yours,

Mary Sachs

December Seventh,
Nineteen thirty-two.

Original portrait of
Miss Sachs by Kublenov
destroyed in fire — re-
production by same art-
ist from memory.

Mary's letter to customers in special section of Harrisburg Telegraph.

Mary Sachs was the recipient of many honors.
PA State Archives, MG-297 Mary Sachs Collection.

Mary's Lancaster store. PA State Archives, MG-297.

A young Mary. PA State Archives, MG-297.

Officers of Air Force Intelligence School, housed at Mary's residence during the War. PA State Archives, MG-297.

Mary speaking at dinner of UJCA where the JCC auditorium was named for her. PA State Archives, MG-297.

Interior of 212 Men's Shop, part of Mary Sachs complex.
PA State Archives, MG-297.

Mary Sachs delivery truck. PA State Archives, MG-297.

Portrait of Mary that hangs in JCC auditorium.

THE WOMAN

Mary, who created the business and drove it with her unique entrepreneurial philosophy, certainly was a keen-minded woman who was not held back by her lack of formal education. And hers was a complex personality, evoking strong feelings.

In his unpublished monograph, Robert Crist offers this description of Mary:

> During the 42 years that Mary Sachs was growing to be a formidable presence in Harrisburg, she eluded exact description or easy understanding. She was simple and complex, tender and harsh, generous yet close. Readers of the social pages were treated to her high-minded opinions in a series of institutional advertisements, but others were subject to her harsh language in personal encounters.
>
> To the elite, she was deferential; to common folk, sometimes haughty. At a posh Paris salon, the couturiers might note the serene grand dame; at a loading dock, a deliveryman might brush with a figure in tattered slippers . . .
>
> The man who solicited for a charitable organization in Miss Sachs's generosity, re-appearing as a salesman or supplier, might squirm, when faced with her business acumen . . . Those who recall Mary Sachs a quarter century after her death still mention her stateliness and attribute the effect principally to her erect carriage and upswept coiffure.

Bern Sharfman, author of the previous monograph published by the Trust Fund in 2003, notes that Mary's portrait in the Harrisburg Jewish Community Center auditorium named for her "reflects both kindliness and a regal air."

That would be an adult point of view. Of course, when they were in elementary school in the JCC building, my children—like many of their peers—found Mary's visage to be forbidding. It helped later when a small showcase in the entrance to the auditorium explained who she was and all she had contributed. And that, as said earler, Hannah Sachs Cantor would always provide my children with chocolate kisses whenever we met.

Then Treasurer of the United States Ivy Baker Priest wrote to Edythe Gross, at the store, upon hearing of Mary's death: "She was such a wonderful person. She was a great public-spirited figure and a woman with a deep sense of human values and human worth."

To others, the blend of toughness and kindness they saw in Mary could be baffling.

As noted earlier, Sam Feinberg of *Women's Wear Daily* mentioned that latter quality, as well, in his 1954 series of articles about the Mary Sachs Shops.

"Mary Sachs is matronly in appearance with gray hair with an upswept coiffure," he wrote. "Miss Sachs is concerned about her people quite in the manner of a benevolent despot. When an employee is ill or in other trouble, she wants to know about it. When financial assistance is required, she takes care of the need confidentially."

Mary Sachs never married but had been engaged once to a man from New York with whom she communicated through several letters. (His name was not shared, etc.) But for whatever reason, the family did not like him, and the relationship did not continue.

A newspaper clip at the Historical Society of Dauphin County did reveal the man's name as E. Joy Morris of Philadelphia, a publicity manager for the First International Newspaper and Magazine Syndicate. His father, of the same name, was identified as the inventor and manufacturer of the present-day carousel or merry-go-round (and has a presence on the Internet).

Beyond that, the newspaper called Mary "one of the city's leading business women."

Still, she had qualities that attracted male friends. Rabbi Philip David Bookstaber, her spiritual leader at Temple Ohev Sholom, Harrisburg's Reform Jewish temple, was one. They were very close, and rumormongers insisted there was something more romantic than mere friendship involved. This was something Hannah denied, asserting that "They. Were. Good. Friends. Period."

Others claim that Bookstaber had lost a wife and children in the flu epidemic of 1918 and had no wish to remarry. Still others said that Mary harbored romantic feelings toward the rabbi that he did not share. Probably, with all the principals gone, the truth will never be known.

That there was an emotional connection seems evident. In one impassioned letter Bookstaber sent to Mary on April 6, 1942, he wrote: "Whatever your sensitiveness marks as a hurt may not result of a willingness to hurt on my part; I give you the benefit of that freedom in hurts to my sensitiveness too. The Mary Sachs 'Symphony in C Major' has many cadences and movements; it would be a sorry and unsuccessful symphony if it were in a monotone."

Thanks to what was at least a close friendship with Bookstaber, another relationship of Mary's came to light. At a party in New York City, Mary met an advertising executive of some note. When she returned to Harrisburg, she found a letter from him stating that he had been very impressed by their conversation and hoped she wouldn't object to his writing to her on occasion. A series of letters followed from the widower, ranging from philosophy to current events to religion to sex and to the arts.

Believing that those letters deserved a wider audience, Rabbi Bookstaber prevailed upon Mary to let him edit a volume of them. The book, *The Mary Letters*, came out after the advertising man, identified only as "I.S.J." in the book, had passed away. One Harrisburger who tried to buy a copy over the Internet in 2001 received price quotes ranging from $40 to $50 for a second-hand copy.

Fellow retailer Dick Goldsmith, who knew Mary well and who himself attended dinners at Mary's home—which he called a "beautiful place" that his father helped furnish—was impressed by the type of guests Mary attracted.

"One night," he recalled, "I had Pennsylvania Governor George Leader to the left of me and actor Burgess Meredith to the right. I went up there to listen. The conversation was tremendous. She surrounded herself with interesting people. She was a dominant personality. When Mary spoke, people listened. She had a great brain on her shoulders and was one of the greatest females who ever walked the streets of Harrisburg."

Mary had opened her home as a patriotic gesture of kindness during World War II. She housed up to 18 servicemen at a time while they were attending the nearby Air Force Intelligence School. The school was on the former site of the Harrisburg Academy, a private school K-12 in the area and the current site of the Dixon University Center, headquarters of the Pennsylvania State System of Higher Education.

The guest book Mary asked these servicemen to sign contains the names of some who would become major celebrities—Meredith and fellow actor Gilbert Roland; writer Quentin Reynolds; and producer-director Joshua Logan.

On the front page of the guest book Mary had written: "We welcome you with the wish that you find here the warmth and friendliness of home. Regard it so and, on Sundays, join us at breakfast, brunch or dinner as the case may be. Our rules are few, our one requirement being a record of long distance phone calls, which you will leave with the houseman. Other than that, at ease, gentlemen. Mary Sachs."

Another distinguished guest on an international scale was the late and powerfully articulate Israeli Ambassador to the UN, Abba Eban. When Hannah was in Israel and spotted the Ambassador, at the urging of Frances Goldberg, she went over to speak with him. Of course, he knew her instantly. "'Mary Sachs. Harrisburg,' he reportedly said.

Regardless of what Mary's relationship was with the Rabbi, according to *The Jews of Harrisburg* by Coleman, when Bookstaber published his book *Judaism and the American Mind in Theory and Practice*, which came out in 1938, he dedicated it to: "Mary Sachs, A Woman of Valor and Exponent of the Prophets of Israel."

Not everyone felt the same way about Mary. She was closer to some family members than to others, and one younger relative, speaking on condition of anonymity, told me she was "scared stiff" of Mary, whom she found "not easy."

But she admitted that Mary had obtained "the best doctors" for her, a sickly child.

The late Rabbi David Silver, longtime spiritual leader of Kesher Israel Congregation in Harrisburg, the Orthodox synagogue Mary's mother attended, would say when asked about Mary:

"Others talk about her business success and her money, but I like to talk about her character. Unlike many children, she did not act ashamed of her mother's accent or traditional religious views. Once, when entertaining Pennsylvania Governor and Mrs. Gifford Pinchot on a Friday night before his lecture at her Temple, she invited them to a traditional Sabbath dinner at her mother's home. That's character."

Others would recall that only Mrs. Pinchot attended that meal, but the story is valid nonetheless. When Rabbi Silver told it at the dinner officially naming the Jewish Community Center auditorium after Mary Sachs, one month before her death, she wrote to thank him for bringing her mother's memory into that room.

We also know that Mary wrote to a different Pennsylvania Governor and First Lady, Mr. and Mrs. George M. Leader, inviting them and their children to a Passover Seder.

Mary, according to Paul Beers, was an egalitarian. "Governors' wives shopped in her store, but they were given no more than the same courteous attention anyone else received," he wrote. "The vibrant Cordelia Pinchot was especially fond of her."

Mary had strong feelings, and evoked them as well. While many noted her keen intelligence, charitable endeavors, and business acumen, and the fact that she ran a beautiful store, others pointed to a kind of inflexibility.

Still others noted both her positive and difficult qualities.

One such person was Harold Leibenson, whose wife, Elayne, had worked for Mary years ago before the couple was married. He asserted that the businesswoman was a difficult woman: "If you didn't do it Mary's way, you didn't do it," he said.

Leibenson, who used to buy his clothes at the 212 Men's Shop when it was run by George Friedman, also called Mary a workaholic, someone who traveled for business but probably wouldn't have gone to Paris or NY otherwise.

On the other hand, in his words, her store was "the in place to be for Jewish women," in addition to the Junior Dress Shop, run by Rebecca Golumbic (wife of Philip Garonzik).

"She was a very different kind of person," Leibenson continued. "A single woman, a great lady." Her singleness, in addition to her talent, made Mary "different." "She was very bright, a good businesswoman, with a beautiful store, and she was sharp."

Mary didn't marry, but she encouraged her younger sister Hannah (the youngest in the family) to do so. In a February 17, 1997, article in *The Patriot-News*, writer Sandy Marrone said that the sister's lives were so "intertwined" that Cantor hesitated marrying the shoe store owner she loved until she was assured that Mary would be all right and told her to get married.

"She gave me a black Russian broad tail fur jacket for a wedding present and told me that if I ever wanted to hurt her, I should be unkind to Ben," Hannah told Marrone.

In one of her emotional letters (dated December 31, 1946), Mary wrote to Hannah and Ben on the occasion of their anniversary: "One of the contributing factors, which is most important of all, towards happiness in marriage is the complete understanding of your physical workings . . . in your case, Hannah and Ben, in those blessed years of your marriage, you have had [an] open house with plenty of windows to let in the sun—in fact, all kinds of rays, therefore, out of all that you are the envy of most married couples."

Knowing, perhaps, her own nature, Mary blessed the couple with "continued health and strength to help you 'weather' my storms from time to time."

Although it is not known whether Mary spoke openly about her reasons for remaining single, this letter to Hannah and Ben may shed light on the "storms" that may have played a part.

Mary had also been close to Al Hursh, a Federation leader. "If you gave money to charity, she liked you," Leibenson said.

He and his wife were good friends of Hannah's, and often took her to dinner.

"But Hannah put Mary on a pedestal—you couldn't say anything [negative] to her about Mary," he added.

Another employee of the store passed away recently (May 22, 2014), but had shared her impressions of the woman with Patsy Sympson at The Rose radio station in Lancaster. Sympson had been visiting her with meals-on-wheels.

Sara E. "Betty" Ogelsby of Harrisburg was an artist, especially of oil painting and sketching, who co-owned an art studio on the West Shore and also worked for Mary Sachs as a very young woman dressing windows.

When Ogelsby got married, she told Sympson, Mary kindly bought her a cake and wedding dress and gave her "other things." "She was very generous," Ogelsby added.

At times, though, Mary could be arbitrary.

When actuary Conrad M. Siegel came to Harrisburg in 1959, he worked with Pension Trust Advisory Services, a division of Yoffee & Beitman Insurance Co., which handled the Mary Sachs Pension Plan.

"She had started the plan during World War II because she was worried about her long-term employees and because it was advantageous tax-wise due to the confiscatory tax rate then on profits," he explained.

He recalls a meeting with Mary one Sunday morning in the basement of her building where she was unpacking goods while wearing a rag of a dress.

"Our discussion had to do with two retired employees on pension," said Siegel, who went on to head his own firm. "Back then, you could put a non-compete clause in a pension plan which would eliminate the pension for someone who's going into competition with you. That provision was outlawed in 1974.

"These employees had written to Mary about proposed activities, wondering if they could be considered competitive. One woman, who had moved down to Florida, wanted to take a job as a salesperson with a dress shop in Florida. Mary decided that her territory was the whole country; therefore, she told her it would be considered competitive. The second, a tailor who had moved into an old age home in Philadelphia, had been asked by people in the home to do some alterations for them. Mary ruled that would not be competitive."

In an interview for the Penn State University collection, Sally (Mrs. Albert) Lehrman, of a very prominent Jewish family in Harrisburg, recalled shopping in the Mary Sachs store as a young, married woman, in 1942-1943.

Although Mary was, according to Lehrman, not universally loved by everyone, she recalled that Mary was civic minded and did marvelous things for a lot of people. "She went to bat for Jews fighting quotas and for Jews wanting to be admitted to the staff of Polyclinic Hospital in Harrisburg. She was also the single largest giver in the community, once giving $10,000 to top the largest donation otherwise."

In contrast to some individuals in the community, Mary was "always a Zionist," Lehrman added. "One time I got a call from her, and she was very upset that I hadn't joined Hadassah. I told her there was a personal reason, and she said, 'You've just got to join.'"

Lehrman felt that Mary got back when she gave, because she received "a kick" out of having servicemen celebrities in her home during World War II, as much as they gained from it.

In one of the ads she took out in *The Patriot-News*, Mary paid tribute to Hadassah, "the hand that heals," on the occasion of its Jubilee anniversary.

She called the Hadassah Medical Center, though still evolving from a building point of view, "already a landmark in the humanity of Israel," which reaches out "to the hapless victims of affliction and oppression wherever situated of all races and creeds, with a non-partisan character dedicated to the democratic tradition and equality for all."

Mary also called Hadassah "a great sanctuary of compassion and hope."

Ironically, though, for all her support of institutions in Israel, Mary did not visit the country, unlike her friend Eleanor Roosevelt.

With her strong support of Israel, Mary probably would have enjoyed the fact that in May 1984, when Israel Bonds honored her posthumously, the dinner featured Israel's top designers, such as Beged Or and Gottex.

Yet, with all her positive sides, Mary also could be imperious.

Lehrman said that "Whatever Mary did, it was not done with humility. She'd tell you the fine deeds she did herself."

On the other hand, she admitted, the founder of the Mary Sachs Store did "revolutionize retail."

Decades later, Annette Berman was still rankled by memories of a meeting with her.

Berman had come to the United States in 1948, a French war bride brought by her husband to Middletown, where she working as a teacher.

"After a few months, I received a call from Miss Sachs's secretary, who told me Miss Sachs would like to see me," Berman recalled.

"I was intrigued," she continued. "I had survived the Holocaust, and Miss Sachs was then head of the United

Jewish Appeal locally. I thought she wanted to talk with me about helping with the campaign.

"We made an appointment and I went, though it was difficult, since I did not drive and had to take a bus. I sat and waited and was told, 'Miss Sachs is too busy to see you today.' I came back two days later and was in Miss Sachs's office. She looked me over from toe to head and back again, then said to me, 'Well, I guess you're pretty enough and you speak pretty well. I want you to work in my store.' I was flabbergasted and told her I had a job. 'I know,' she said, 'but I want you to be at my perfume counter.'"

Berman said she thought being a salesgirl was not up to the status of being a teacher but asked nonetheless how much the job would pay.

"Miss Sachs replied, 'Well $20 a week," Berman continued. 'And I said, well, I'm making $25 a week now.' She looked at me and said, 'You know, to work in my store is an honor. I know lots of people who would work for nothing.' I said I wasn't interested, and that was the end of the conversation."

Berman assumed that an article in the newspaper about French war brides coming here had attracted Mary's attention or maybe someone had mentioned her name. Years later Berman bridled at thoughts of that meeting.

"I still get irked when people sanctify her," she added.

Paul Hoch, one of Mary's great-nephews, remembers visiting Sachs when she still lived on Green Street. He also would stop by to see "Aunt Mary" when he went to the store, where his grandfather and grandmother worked. "We weren't that close," he said. "My immediate family was somewhat estranged from the rest of the family, because my grandmother had married a Lutheran.

"I was like 18-19 when she passed away," Hoch continued. "She was always busy. But I was always welcome in the store, and could get whatever I wanted. I do recall going into the store in Harrisburg as a kid and running into my great-aunt in the receiving area; it was very evident she was in charge."

In contrast, Mary's brother Morris, he said, would stop whatever he was doing and spend time with the young man when Hoch visited the store.

His mother, Dorothy Kramer Hoch, describes Mary as "a very regal saleswoman."

Niece Rachel Katzen, who once worked in the Harrisburg store, remembers Mary as having "a great sense of humor; she'd get over her anger fast. The next minute she wouldn't even remember that she had been angry."

Barbara Steinsnyder, of Lancaster, a niece of Hannah and Ben Cantor, knew Mary when Barbara was a child.

"We went and ate dinner with her," she recalled. "I was most impressed with her when young. I loved to hear her tell stories about how she grew up and about the business."

Hoch had feelings about what made his great-aunt successful. "She had a very special concept and made her clients feel special," he said. "She had trucks with 'Mary Sachs' on them and not much inventory. But she would say to a client, 'I have just the dress for you.'"

Despite the lack of closeness between him and his great-aunt, he said he respected Mary for "working so hard and being so successful. The store was classy." He recalls the employee cafeteria, beauty spa downstairs, an elevator with an operator, and switchboard operator with plug-ins.

Moreover, Hoch added, "She made it classy. That's the way she was, although she was a very plain lady, personally."

He also cited her generosity. When his grandfather, Anthony Kramer, died, Mary "made sure" his grandmother, Lena, who had worked in the children's department, was well taken care of. His grandfather ran the print shop downstairs, which included making Mary's own shopping bags, advertisements, cards, and monogramming.

Add feistiness to the characteristics that welled up in Mary. Once invited to dine with her friend Rabbi Bookstaber at a table of Harrisburgers where he was being honored by City College of New York with an alumni medal, Mary turned him down.

"Please forgive me, Rabbi," she wrote. "I have a feeling that you will more than understand the predicament I would be in if I had to break bread with most of those people. I know they are not my friends."

On the other hand, people of note bestowed many honors on Mary.

On July 14, 1958, then U.S. Senator Edward Martin of Pennsylvania entered into the *Congressional Record* an article from *Commonwealth Magazine*, entitled "Mary Sachs: Merchant Princess." That became her nom de plume.

The reason Martin bestowed the name, he said, is that "The story is so interesting and could be so inspiring to many of our young people."

Eleanor Roosevelt once devoted the bulk of one of her "My Day" columns, which appeared in papers six days a week, to Mary.

She wrote that during a visit to Harrisburg, she had met Miss Sachs, whom she found to be "hospitable, warm and has a philosophy that filled me with admiration. She is a businesswoman who has never married but she loves children . . . I surmise she has been inspiring others through her own generosity to be as generous as possible. However, I imagine few can even match her."

Mrs. Roosevelt visited Mary's home sometime in the early part of 1960, and on March 25, wrote to her: "This is just a note to thank you again for all your kindness. You were good to welcome me so warmly, and I want you to know that I very much enjoyed meeting you."

Morton Spector, who was acquainted both with the Mary Sachs retail clothing stores and the founder's involvement in many local charities, recalls her generosity and leadership qualities.

"She was a Champion for the State of Israel, which became a state in 1948, and was a leader in giving to the United Jewish Appeal, in support of Israel," he said. "She not only gave willingly to these causes, but also lent her home for many fund-raising events, some of which I attended."

After an illness, Mary wrote a group letter on February 21, 1953, on behalf of Israel Bonds: "I don't think anyone can answer questions intelligently about the State of Israel except the unfortunate men and women and children who have benefited - through homelessness, through lack of medication, through lack of security anywhere on earth, and the one place they seem to be able to go and be accepted with welcome exchange on the part of the residents of Israel . . ."

When she made a pledge to an organization, Spector continued, she paid it immediately, whether she had the money or not. She did this by borrowing, or taking bank loans, so the charity would have its funds right away.

Those who met Mary, whatever they thought, seemed to have formed lasting impressions about her. Another Mary (Bradley), long associated with *The Patriot-News*, Harrisburg's daily, was writing about Mary as late as 2005 and 2007.

Still another insight into the complex Mary Sachs character came at her funeral service. Everett R. Clinchy, then president of the World Brotherhood, stated:

"We will always remember Miss Sachs as an interesting, colorful personality. She could get furiously indignant about human stupidity and evil, and could excoriate the folly and the phony in man . . . but she would soon exercise her delightful gifts of humor that gave balance to her life."

Kenneth Collins, the columnist, wrote after Mary's death: "In this age of conformity, it is challenging to meet the stimulus of a unique personality. Miss Sachs and her vanities, her crotchetiness, her moments of exasperation, her errors of judgment. She was not always filled with sweetness and light. Who among us is?"

"But beneath the very human failing were exceptional virtues," he added.

Two months before her death, former Governor and U.S. Senator Martin wrote in a letter:

"Miss Sachs is a real American in every sense of the word. In all her relations to mankind, she has exemplified

America at its best . . . there is no honor too great for this person."

But many in the extended Sachs family harbored deep resentment bordering on anger because of their perception that Mary devoted so many of her assets to charitable causes and ignored family needs. At the very least, their argument goes, for someone so interested in education, Mary (and later Hannah) should have provided for the education of the next generation of Sachses.

"Mary did offer anyone in my mother's generation a college education," Greenberg said, "and my mother was the only one who took her up on it. I wouldn't fault Aunt Mary for that."

His mother went to Hood College and became a social worker, like his father.

Mary was William Greenberg's great-aunt. (Her sister, Emma Katzen, was his grandmother.) An attorney originally based in Newark and living in Princeton (but now a federal judge in DC), Greenberg serves as head of the Mary Sachs Trust.

His wife is related to the Kaufmanns, owners of a large department store. He was familiar with the pattern in American Jewish history of Jews who opened and owned department stores and used their wealth to be philanthropists.

"She was the matriarch of the family," he recalled of Mary. "She was a moral example. I worked for a while in the store in the late '50s. She was a businesswoman who cared greatly about details, who was innovative, who was willing to take risks on the one hand and at the same time never went beyond the basic conservative views of her clientele."

Greenberg recalls working at the store one summer for a modest salary just to learn about business.

"Mary said, 'I'll outfit you for school; pick out what you want,'" he said. "I remember getting a few shirts and five pair of khaki chino pants. She said, 'Why would you get five of the same thing?' I told her, 'This is the only kind the kids wear.' Price wasn't the object for her; the redundancy of it was."

Greenberg offered this view of family feelings: "Mary was the economic provider for much of the family of her generation, the generation before her—her mother and father—and the next generation," he explained. "She had a different outlook, owning the fanciest store in Central Pennsylvania but being fairly frugal with herself.

"She did have a fancy house, a driver and butler and a cook," he continued. "She was generous with her money to charity. I think people in the family who worked for her and didn't get paid a lot expected some kind of additional reward. Mary did offer anyone in my mother's generation a college education, and my mother was the only one who took her up on it. I wouldn't fault Aunt Mary for that."

"Not a flashy person," Mary was "progressive" toward her employees, he added.

His parents got married in Mary's home in 1937. And every time he visited the store, she'd tell him to pick out whatever he wanted and she'd pick up the tab. Unfortunately, Greenberg said, he couldn't afford to shop there regularly on his own.

Donehoo declared the store as an "establishment which has through its unique methods achieved national distinction" and whose story reads like an Horatio Alger, "except that Miss Sachs' progress was for some years marked by discouraging obstacles."

Greenberg also affirmed that Mary could engender strong emotions in people.

Peter Wambach, at the time a noted Harrisburg broadcaster, writer, personality, and speechwriter for Pennsylvania's Lieutenant Governor, wrote an eloquent letter to the Sachs family when Mary died.

"God, in his many beneficiaries to us," he wrote, "sometimes gives us certain privileges . . . and you, my friends, were privileged to live with 'my dear lady.' In the small body of Mary Sachs was the love of God Himself, lavished upon you to whom she was so close. It was a privilege, which I often secretly wished to have been mine, to be even closer to her than I was privileged to be . . . She would tell me on occasions that 'I have never been a mother,' but in that she was wrong. Ask the thousands of lame and ill, ask the hundreds of youths, ask the unsung millions of Israelis, and those who are motherless in times when they need mothers, and they will tell you that Mary Sachs was indeed Mother to the Motherless."

Years after her death, *The Patriot News* columnist Paul Beers wrote about Mary:

> "Mary Sachs was small of stature, maybe 5-foot-2, but she was an energetic woman . . . She was humble and simple, and she admired that in people and in fashion . . . She admired precise thinking and originality, and sought those qualities . . . Miss Sachs' influence is so great that it is impossible to imagine a Harrisburg without her being here."

Mary's life, noted Bern Sharfman in the original edition of this book, "inspired excess at times." He further wrote: "Mary may not have been the saint sister Hannah elevated her memory to in adulation, but on balance, human flaws and all, her commercial achievements and her charitable instincts set a high standard."

Hannah would often repeat this sentence: "Mother said of Mary, 'She has been the mother and father to everyone in the family.'"

For her part, in 1941, Mary wrote at Hannah and Ben's New Year's Eve anniversary: ". . . Somehow or other I treasure you. I suppose it was because you were the last born and were the baby of the family. I pride myself that you are my baby and Ben is simply sharing you with me."

The father of Bruce Friedman worked for Mary Sachs for 30 years, running the men's department, after leaving a position at Allan Stuart, another men's store. "My parents were married in her home; I have a picture of it," he said. "She was a real mentor. He would have called her a grand old lady of old-time retail, a very formal person and very philanthropic."

Many people noted Mary's singleness, which definitely made her stand out more than she would have today. Many Jewish women entrepreneurs in the 20th century were married and had families in addition to their enterprises, even if sometimes divorce followed later. "She was married to the store," said Friedman.

Mary also demanded hard work from others. "My dad worked his tush off six days a week, and sometimes Sundays if she needed him on Sundays," Friedman said. "She was fair but demanding."

Bob Seidenberg recalls "being taken" to Mary Sachs Store by his mother, Sylvia, who had a "keen sense of style, true to her New York roots."

He also remembers going upstairs, where he would be fitted for one type of shoe—Bally's. "It seemed to take hours, with the shoe man commenting and my mother overseeing—a level of attention that has long disappeared. I don't think I realized how high-end a shoe it was until I was doing window-shopping, much later, in Chicago."

Seidenberg still has a natty orange blazer bought from Sachs's 212 Men's Shop.

Service went beyond the store premises. He recalls a "sweet-faced little guy" named Richie, who was Mary's deliveryman at one point. "He made frequent trips to our house and my grandmother's, due to my mother's shopping proclivity."

Several people mentioned the Mary Sachs trucks, which were apparently a novelty then.

Allan Stuart started the 212 Men's Shop in the early 1930s on Strawberry Alley behind the Penn Harris Hotel. It was a "little hole in the wall," said his son, Jeb. Then he went into partnership with Byron Crego in a shoe store. "It was a model; people wanted to come."

Stuart sold his partner his inventory before serving in the war, and Crego didn't sell it back. Mary Sachs had been a friend of the family and of his grandparents. "Everyone then knew everybody, whether on the Hill or Uptown," said Jeb Stuart. "Mary wanted to open a men's department, in

1946. Dad sold her on the idea. They opened it on Cranberry Court, as part of the Mary Sachs complex."

In time, Mary's store would span the entire block of North Third Street in Harrisburg. Only a few years later, in 1950, Stuart left Mary Sachs and started his own business. "She was very upset," Jeb Stuart recalled. "He had very high-end clothing and quite a following. His motto was, 'You can't have it until it fits.' He complemented Mary's [emphasis on] quality."

The 212 Shop, as the men's department was called, was featured in *Apparel* magazine, published by Esquire, in July 1948.

Mary's relationship with his father was as partners, not employee to employer, Stuart noted. "She loved him, and gave him free rein."

In the epic work, *Building Harrisburg: The Architects and Builders, 1719-1941*, author Ken Frew wrote that Mary was eager to have her store "reflect New York." She approached Charles Howard Lloyd, the most prominent Harrisburg architect of the time, asking him to accompany her to New York's elegant Fifth Avenue to see if there was a building she liked.

After he turned her down—apparently for lack of time, Frew speculated—she next approached Lawrie & Green and Ray Shoemaker instead; they got the job.

The store, which at first had only one story and a mezzanine, "was quite unlike anything in the city," Frew, a historian at the Historical Society of Dauphin County, continued. Ed Green billed his design as of "Italian precedent," with a striking mix of Romanesque and Classical style influences.

According to Frew, the interior of the store was patterned after the J. P. Hollander Company department store on New York's Fifth Avenue, at 3 East 57 Street. Mary engaged the decorators responsible, Eleanor Le Maire and John Weber, to work with the architects. She also hired both firms when adding two additional stories to the building in 1937.

"It was just what I was looking for," she told the *Harrisburg Telegraph*. "Somehow I felt that I had helped plan that store."

Dr. Donald Freedman, a retired physician, called Mary Sachs "the first Lady of Harrisburg," by far. "She led the league of Harrisburg Jewry—by being the first of everything," he said." She was clever and smart, and whenever something had to be done, she was part of it. She had a way about her. People followed her."

Freedman further stated that one hears about men who were "big about community," but Mary was bigger. "She could do things nobody could do," he said. "The community dwindled after she passed away."

That same can-do attitude reflected in Mary's magnificent store, which was the store of Harrisburg, the city's nicest store, Freedman said. "She became a pioneer. It had pizazz, and was prestigious. It was a status symbol to carry a shopping bag or hatbox from Mary Sachs; it was like a Bergdorf or Bloomingdale's."

If Mary was charitable, she was also frugal. Freedman recalled that Mary and Hannah (or another sister) would go into New York by train and sit on a bench to eat dinner, which they had brought along.

Fannie Krevsky found Mary Sachs a "fascinating woman." She was particularly impressed that Mary opened her house to the military during World War II, and that she took good care of her sisters, Zelda and Rachel.

"Her largesse with the center was legendary," added Krevsky, referring to the Jewish Community Center.

Krevsky also asserted that Mary's influence went beyond central Pennsylvania—that the Neiman Marcus Store in Dallas is fashioned after hers.

"The fact that someone made such strides with no education was miraculous," she added. "It was rags to riches, humility (in the sense of humble beginnings) to hauteur."

While others found a certain coldness in Mary, Krevsky recalled her "wandering through the store, with no airs about her."

She would ask customers, like Krevsky herself, if they had found what they wanted, and if everything was all right.

Lee Anthony, who was in charge of retail advertising at *The Patriot-News*, was assigned to Mary Sachs in 1940 and was outspoken about what dealing with her was like.

"She was a boss," he said. "If she didn't like something, she didn't like it," he said. "But she was a very good teacher. I learned a lot from her."

You couldn't make a change to the ads the Fletcher Company prepared without her noticing, Anthony added.

Mary was also extraordinarily generous in certain ways, he said, though claiming she didn't pay her employees well.

The topics in the ad-essays were emblematic of Mary's sharp mind and breadth of interest. As noted above, once she devoted an entire ad to how dirty the trains were—she took them often between Harrisburg and New York. The ads were half-pages, with no photographs.

There was another connection between Anthony and Mary Sachs: Lee's father, Edgar, was assistant manager at Mary's store and took care of the boy's department when it opened. "Mary would go on vacation and she'd give him extra money."

On the other hand, Anthony recalls, Morris, Mary's brother, who worked at the store, was very helpful to everyone.

Anthony explained that Mary was easily insulted, and you had to be careful to use the "right words." And she could be demanding.

Sometimes she would call him at 4 or 5 in the morning at home—people who worked for her were her "property," he said. When Anthony mentioned her early-morning calls to his boss, he said to tell Mary that the next time she did that, he would charge her advertising rates.

On one occasion, after Anthony contradicted Mary and used the wrong expression, she threw him out of the store and told him not to use the front door after that. One day he ran into her in the receiving department, throwing shirts around. She asked why he had come in through that door, and he reminded her of the previous incident.

"Mary said she wouldn't have said that," Anthony recalled. "From then on, everything was OK. The biggest problem was you had to tiptoe round her. Basically, she was a very humble person with no airs. Sometimes she came to the store in a nightgown, slippers, and bathrobe, but no one could put anything on her."

Her store was also one of the first businesses to have a pension plan, funded from the parking garage. As mentioned, there was a lunchroom for employees. And the store seemed to have been run on "the up and up," Anthony added. "Never was there any bad stuff that came out about them."

In one ad, devoted to Father's Day, Mary paid tribute to Allan Stuart not for being a fine merchant "responsible for the growing prestige of a fine Shop for Men" but for his devotion to his family—which Mary called "the true test of a man." She spoke of his being a fine father to Little Ann.

Another holiday-related ad was in honor of Labor Day, in which the hard-working Mary paid tribute to labor and called her adopted land "the most wonderful country in the world." She also spoke of the "the courage and the means to correct all errors" as the source of American strength.

That same Labor Day-related ad spoke of labor as being "highly regarded, honored and respected" in this country.

She might have been expressing her own philosophy.

The Evening News of Harrisburg reported that a writer from *System*, "a well-known business magazine published in Chicago," came to visit the Harrisburg store. The article he wrote for the magazine focused on how a business could reduce expenses "to give more service."

According to the reporter (whose name isn't given), among the factors to which Mary Sachs attributed the reduction of expenses, were: Lowered rent expenses through doing a large volume of business in a store 22' by 110'; decreased selling expense, through providing a selling arrangement in the store enabling her force to attain the maximum in selling power; buying of merchandise with a thought devoted in many instances to possible customers for the garments under consideration; encouraging morning shopping, thus distributing the peak load and making possible the handling of 50 percent more business with the same force; and finally, advantages of keeping stock in an inaccessible stock room.

According to Morton Spector, the Mary Sachs store had the latest fashions from New York's garment district. "Although Harrisburg boasted a vibrant shopping community, she was thought of as the 'Merchant Princess,'" he wrote. "Many governors and their wives and other local political figures patronized her stores."

The clothing also had a special Mary Sachs label, though sometimes designer labels were in there too, said Alyce Spector.

Some people remember the store more than the woman who owned and ran it. Eleanor (Elie) Allen loved to shop there. The wedding dress she had obtained there was exhibited in the 2012 exhibit at Strawberry Square by the Historical Society of Dauphin County.

"I shopped there before and after my marriage in 1949 until the store closed," Allen, the widow of Heath Allen, recalled. "I knew I would get what I wanted. The store was very accommodating."

Allen still has her wedding dress up in a cedar closet. "It was a beautiful, beautiful dress," she said. Although sad when the store closed, she said she "adjusted," and since then has shopped "wherever." But she did miss the personal touch of the Mary Sachs store.

The 1931 City Directory indicated not only Mary's clothing store but also several others, including Feller's, Kaufmans, Pomeroy's, and Bowman's.

One indication, though, of Mary's status among all of these was the large story published in the *Harrisburg Telegraph* that she would be building again after the fire that year. It included an architect's sketch of the new store.

The article also mentioned that Mr. Shoemaker, "the good neighbor," in Mary's words, opened his Harrisburger Hotel to her after the fire and did everything in his power to assist her and to the tenants forced into the street by the fire.

According to the paper, Mary said, "Insofar as possible all materials will be bought in Harrisburg; Harrisburg workmen will be favored. After all is said and done, Harrisburg is able to furnish almost all that is needed in the way of rebuilding."

Lee Anthony cited another sign of Mary's generosity. When his father bought his first house, Mary asked where he had gotten the money and was upset he had gone to the bank rather than coming to her for help. She paid the bank off, taking a little from his bank account gradually till he had paid her off.

As stated earlier, many prominent people would stay in Mary's home, which Anthony also described as "beautiful." But despite a maid, chauffeur, and maintenance guys, she would have been "embarrassed" to have it called a mansion.

The home, a five-bay, stone-constructed, neo-Georgian dwelling (as described by the Historic Harrisburg Association), was completed in 1926 for Ira P. Romberger, president of Cort and Company. In 1935, Mary acquired the home, where she lived till her death in 1960.

The home featured a high-hipped roof assembly, pedimented main entrance frontispiece supported by columns, and soldier-coursed window lintels, as further described by HHA.

"An unusual feature of the house," wrote the Association, "is its symmetrical through-dormer chimney configurations on the house's north and south elevations."

Paul Hoch, a member of the Trust and family member, wasn't that close to Mary, though he recalls visiting the store. His grandfather and grandmother worked there; he was like only 18 or 19 when Mary passed away.

"But I was always welcome in the store and could get whatever I wanted," Hoch said. "I would roam around the store, but she was always busy."

Paul Hoch was also impressed by the big trucks with Mary's name on it that delivered packages. "It was a very special concept and made her clients feel special," Hoch said. "I respected her for working so hard and being so successful. The store was special, classy. She made it classy. It was the way she was."

Mary would go to New York to buy special things; the gift departments were always special.

"But personally," Hoch said," she was a very plain lady. If your ran into her she had a pencil in her hand working on something."

Sometimes on Sundays they would visit Aunt Emma. When his grandfather died, Mary made sure his grandmother was taken care of.

His grandfather ran the print shop: Mary had her own bags, advertisements, cards, and monogramming. There was also a beauty spa downstairs in the store and an elevator with an operator, as well as a switchboard operator.

"In Central Pennsylvania, the names of Mary Sachs and two of her sisters, Hannah Sachs Cantor and Yetta Sachs Carpenter, have earned a place on that roster of past giants," wrote Bern Sharfman.

Pete Wambach referred to Mary, in his "Around the Square" column of December 19, 1982, as "fabled," as a "merchant extraordinaire and peerless philanthropist." He recalled celebrating Passover at the Sachs home with Christians and Muslims.

"That night I heard Mary Sachs speak, as if sermonizing," he wrote, "her theories of 'how to give' (not what or when) and I hope that I have remembered well, for she was the outstanding 'giver' of this community, and influenced my own charitable habits as much as anyone ever has."

An unnamed patron (in Donehoo's history) of Mary's called the entrepreneur's attention to a passage in Ralph Waldo Emerson's essay on "Character," which the patron believed applied to Mary herself: . . . "As soon as you see the natural merchant, who appears not so much a private agent, as her factor and Minister of Commerce, his natural probity combines with his insight into the fabric of society to put him above tricks . . . he inspires respect and the wish to deal with him, both for the quiet spirit of honor which attends him, and for the intellectual pastime which the spectacle of so much ability affords."

Only, of course, in Mary's case it was a "she."

How did Mary Sachs, an immigrant with almost no formal education, become the success that she did? There's always an element of uncertainty in such situations, and luck definitely factors in. It wasn't unusual for immigrants to make rapid progress, even without formal education. Mary was born on March 10, 1988, in Lithuania, then under the control of Russia. If the family had remained in Europe, or had not come to the United States, or even if they had come much later, the world might not have known of Mary Sachs. In fact, there probably would not have been a Mary Sachs.

Reading Matter and Interests

Like her cosmopolitan approach to fashion, her reading tastes were universal.

Mary was a prolific and diverse reader. Among the books in her library were *The Golden Word: A Religion for All Creators of Beauty* and the *Memoirs of Glückel of Hameln*, mentioned elsewhere in this book. She was clearly a role model for Mary (except that Glückel had a family, including several children).

The *Autobiography with Letters of William Lon Phelps*, a lecturer in literature and literary criticism at Yale; *The Great Betrayal*, an expose by Stephen Wise and Jacob de Haas about the White Paper restricting Jewish immigration to pre-State of Israel Palestine; and *Judaism and the American Mind in Theory and Practice* by her dear friend and mentor Philip David Bookstaber were also among her books. The latter, as noted elsewhere, was dedicated to Mary.

Another book, *For the Life of Me*, the autobiography of Robert Briscoe, the first Jewish Mayor of Dublin, Ireland, had the inscription: "With most sincere appreciation for what you have done and continue to do for America and Israel."

Another autobiography was that of prolific American-Jewish author Fannie Hurst, whose novels included the much-filmed *Imitation of Life* and *Back Street*.

The Broader View

Did Mary Sachs and the retail business she launched
and developed in Harrisburg merit broader attention?
Richard (Dick) Goldsmith, then a fellow retailer
in the quality furniture business, still looks back and
concludes, "It was the greatest store Harrisburg ever had.
My mother never had a stitch of clothing on her back that
didn't come from Mary Sachs. They'd travel together on
vacations."

Bern Sharfman recalled his own mother's positive reac-
tion to the store when she visited Harrisburg in 1961. As a
New Yorker who browsed the specialty shops of Manhattan
with regularity, she still was awed, he wrote, "by the ambi-
ance of the place and the quality of the merchandise she
found there."

The national trade media, as well as the local newspaper,
found Mary's business acumen worthy of being discussed
in a broader arena. Here are just a few of the conclusions
drawn by the columnists, fashion experts, and historians
who checked out the Mary Sachs operation.

In his *History of Harrisburg and Dauphin County*, George
P. Donehoo wrote: "Mary Sachs, proprietor of the attractive
woman's specialty shop on North Third Street, Harrisburg,
an establishment which has through its unique methods
achieved national distinction, is an example of the flowering of exceptional commercial talent, under the fostering
influence of a favorable environment . . . She impressed
one as being decidedly surprised and not a little startled
at finding herself at the head of a powerful commercial

enterprise. Others, however, affirm that her success is but the inevitable expression of exceptional ability coupled with a sterling character."

In 1954, *Women's Wear Daily's* Sam Feinberg wrote: "With scores of department and specialty stores capitulating, mentally or physically or both, to the mechanical ways of the chains individualists have become as scarce as the proverbial hen's teeth. Yet, in many cities and towns throughout the country, there are independent retailers, who still stand out from all the rest. Their independence is evidenced by in financial and merchandising control, in selling and advertising, and in relations with resources, customers, employees and the community at large. Such an establishment is Mary Sachs, Inc,, Harrisburg, Pennsylvania, with another shop in Lancaster, Pennsylvania."

In *Commonwealth*: The Magazine for Pennsylvania (1956) the following quote appeared: "The story of Mary Sachs is as full of romance of American business initiative as any that Horatio Alger wrote . . . The name of Mary Sachs, as Pennsylvania women can testify, stands for two of the most beautiful specialty shops in the country—at Harrisburg and Lancaster—and signifies to many thousand of women the finest in clothes."

Kenneth Collins of *Women's Wear Daily* wrote in 1960: "What is so unusual about Miss Sachs and about the store that bears her name? To this question I could give many answers. The store (and its companion shop in Lancaster) is beautiful; the housekeeping is meticulous; the merchandise is lovely; the service is expert; the timing of seasons is faultless. I could go on and on with these statements. All would be true, yet none would answer the query. For there is a special quality about Mary Sachs the woman and about Mary Sachs the store that cannot be summed up in conventional words and phrases. Others may differ with me, but I have my own word for Mary Sachs and for the business that she founded. That word is HEART."

In the Harrisburg *Evening News* (1968) reporter Myron T. Kalina wrote: "Friday is the 50th anniversary of Mary

Sachs Shop—an institution founded on the dream of a poor Jewish girl who turned into a merchant princess. The late Miss Sachs was a tiny woman but she cast a long shadow . . . Mrs. Hannah Cantor, Miss Sachs' sister, who now operates the business, said . . . 'She was a wonderful woman and one who loved Harrisburg.' And Harrisburg loved her."

In the *Evening News* (1982), columnist Paul B. Beers stated: "When Harrisburgers talk about how public endeavors should be managed, of what kind of business this town needs, of how 'a touch of class' should be restored to private life, or who's an appropriate model of achievement for aspiring women, Mary Sachs is cited . . . She was humble and simple, and she admired that in people and in fashion . . . She admired precise thinking and originality."

In her *Central PA* Magazine (1998) article, Yvonne Milspaw wrote: "Long after Mary Sachs' death, her shop is still missed, and is recalled with intensity, admiration and respect. A tremendously successful businesswoman, she embodied the immigrant dream of American opportunity. And as a warm, compelling and genuine personality, she supported the community in ways that benefited almost everyone in Central Pennsylvania."

THE LEGACY

In addition to the other sources cited above, Prof. Simon J. Bronner (of Penn State University), in his *Images of America: Greater Harrisburg's Jewish Community*, lauds Mary "for championing Jewish and humanitarian causes" in addition to her innovative entrepreneurial practices.

The Mary Sachs Forest in Israel was only one of her many contributions to that country.

In June 1981, the Pennsylvania Division of the American Association of University Women undertook a two-year project entitled "Pennsylvania Women in History."

In the resulting volume, *Silhouettes: Women of Harrisburg Remembered*, the AAUW's Pennsylvania Division wrote profiles of non-living women who were born prior to 1930, resided within a 10-mile radius of Harrisburg, and who made significant contributions in their own right.

Among them were educator Anna L. Carter, journalist Lillie Harris, civic leaders Anne and Gertrude McCormick, artist Maya Schock, and musician Margaret Hull.

In the book's dedication, Sally C. Chamberlain, president of the Harrisburg Branch of the AAUW, wrote: "Women have contributed significantly to the growth and development of the Harrisburg community in countless ways and have made notable achievements in a number of professions as well. Yet very little information has been readily available to document the accomplishments of the prominent women of Harrisburg's past."

Specifically of Mary, the book stated: "At a time when women were an extremely small part of the business world, Mary Sachs was a highly successful merchant."

It also pointed out that at her home on Front Street, she entertained "hosts of people from diverse backgrounds—diplomats, attorneys, writers, educators, military personnel, physicians, architects, clothing designers, and manufacturers."

As stated elsewhere in this book, among Mary's favorites were Eleanor Roosevelt, Abba Eban, Fannie Hurst, Quentin Reynolds, and poet Edwin Markham. She boarded such visiting Army students as Broadway director/producer Joshua Logan, and actors Burgess Meredith and Gilbert Roland.

The AAUW publication said of Mary: "Merchandisewise, she was responsible for many innovations: employee pension fund, shopper parking, and gift wrapping."

AAUW stated that: "Admired by all who knew her, Mary Sachs had a philosophy of life which stressed dedication to hard work, high regard for personal responsibility, and a strong sense of morality."

In a September 1998 article in *Central PA* magazine, writer Milspaw remembered Mary Sachs, whose store she visited with her family from their home in Elizabethtown.

Milspaw said she had no difficulty recalling the "peacock-blue velvet of the elegantly cut holiday dress" her mother bought there 40 years ago.

"Long after Mary Sachs's death, her shop is still missed, and is recalled with intensity, admiration and respect," Milspaw noted. "A tremendously successful business-women, she embodied the immigrant dream of American opportunity."

"Sachs wanted the look to evoke upscale New York sophistication, and the result, a mix of Romanesque and classical influences," according to architectural historian Ken Frew, was a "design unlike anything in the city in 1968, the 50th anniversary of the first store. Hannah Sachs Cantor sold it to Hess's, which closed it 10 years later."

Partly, the appreciation of Mary Sachs stemmed from her own appreciation of her adopted city. Although she had also lived in Baltimore and Steelton, she had a "fierce attachment," by her own description and the impressions of others, to Harrisburg.

Mary Sachs and her store made an impression on no less a distinguished and universally known personality than Eleanor Roosevelt, who described a visit to the Harrisburg Jewish community in her six-day-a-week newspaper column "My Day." Mrs. Roosevelt spoke about Mary's philanthropy and community service as well as business acumen, but in addition calling her a "hospitable and warm woman."

Women's Wear Daily columnist Kenneth Collins, in January 1960, asked rhetorically why Mary deserved the adjective "remarkable." "What is so unusual about Miss Sachs and about the store that bears her name," he said.

Donehoo compares Mary's to a "Horatio Alger" story, in terms of success—if not for the "discouraging obstacles" she lived through.

According to Donehoo, Mary's business was doing a volume of more than $600,000 yearly when she was in her 30s. It is ironic, he noted, that many years before that she was permitted to resign "without protest" from a saleswoman's position paying a wage of $5 a week. "Finally, after further discouraging incidents," the historian wrote, "she secured a position as stock-girl in a women's wear shop at $6 weekly." Her move to her own independent business as backed by only $6000.

Despite a strong ego, Mary also had strong principles. In her seventieth year, Robert G. Christ wrote in his unpublished manuscript, after 35 years of membership in Temple Ohev Sholom, she resigned because of a matter of conscience.

After Allan Stuart returned from World War II, he went into partnership with Mary Sachs and opened the 212 Men's Shop on Third Street. He ran the store from 1946 to 1950, when the Commerce Building was completed at Second and Pine Streets. There he opened his own store on the first floor. In addition, Mary Sachs was a "friend of the family," Stuart said.

When Temple Ohev Sholom constructed a Sunday School, Mary stipulated that it be open to nonmembers. Her parents were more Orthodox.

Mary donated money as well to Albert Einstein Medical School, as part of the Founders Hall, in 1957, and to the National Conference of Christians and Jews. The plaque at Einstein's Founders Hill commends Mary and other individuals "whose understanding, vision, and generosity helped to create broader opportunities for medical education and research."

A half-year later (November 9, 1961), *Women's Wear Daily* noted that despite Mary's passing, her influence was "seen still alive in her shops." This was demonstrated, the article continued, by a framed motto hanging on the wall in an office in the Harrisburg store that read: "Times change, but the character of our service remains the same."

Also reflective of Mary's spirit is a section of the foyer of the Harrisburg shop, known as The Founder's Corner. It contained citations and plaques representing the many interests Mary supported generously.

At a1958 dinner, Michael Comay, Israel's chief delegate to the United Nations and ambassador to Great Britain and Canada, honored Mary.

Mary said she sold "fashion, not styles." As an article (November 9, 1961) in *Women's Wear Daily* after her death, explained: "The Mary Sachs objective is to present not stylish clothes, but simple, basically beautiful clothes which derive their charm from good lines and fine workmanship. Fashion rather than faddish styles, keynotes the operation."

Marilyn Kanenson, a community leader, recalled the store as "beautiful, open, lavish, elegant, and very New York-ish." "You could get anything you wanted," she said. "And if they didn't have it, they would get it. The salespeople were great."

Looking back with sadness, as many others have done since, Kanenson said that when Hannah was getting old, and the store "had passed its time," it was time to sell it.

"Downtown had changed dramatically [at the time)," she said. "People didn't go."

Alyce Spector agreed. Malls were opening, and Harrisburg was in the doldrums. Downtown was like a ghost town.

In March 1960, former First Lady Eleanor Roosevelt wrote this item in her nationally syndicated column, "My Day": "I went to Harrisburg, Pa., yesterday afternoon to speak for the United Jewish Appeal, and there I met a very remarkable woman. Her name is Miss Mary Sachs."

Sachs died a few months after Roosevelt penned that column, but she left a legacy of philanthropy, of generosity in spirit as well as wealth—". . . she gave to countless organizations, from hospitals and the Boy Scouts to religious institutions and colleges," states a collection of documents from the Pennsylvania State Archives.

In *The Jews of Harrisburg*, Michael Coleman devotes a section to Rabbi Philip D. Bookstaber, Mary's good friend and spiritual leader of Temple Ohev Sholom. He then goes on to describe Mary, stating that Bookstaber's dedication to Mary in his book *Judaism and the American Mind in Theory and Practice* "accurately" assesses "this remarkable individual who rose from lowly immigrant to successful businesswoman and philanthropist" and was "an inspiration to others."

Mary was part of a period of growth of Jewish business that occurred from 1917 to 1929, said Coleman. The War, he noted sadly, was a "boom to the economy." "The growth of businesses owned by Jews in Harrisburg paralleled the fortunes of many non-Jewish-owned concerns. They suffered the same vicissitudes as others, and there were success stories as well as failures."

Among the success stories were that of Louis Lehrman, who came to New York City from Russia in 1886. Sam and Louis Lehrman started the Harrisburg Grocery Company and later Louis Lehrman and Sons, from which the Rite Aid Corporation developed.

THE CHARITABLE INSTINCT

Mary Sachs not only had a clear philosophy of how to do business; she also had a clear, persistent philosophy of charity. Sometimes, she would express it in capsulated form.

As *Patriot-News* reporter Myron T. Kalina quoted her posthumously in a 1968 article commemorating the 50th anniversary of the Mary Sachs Shop, "Some people collect paintings and other valuables; I am a collector of helping."

Patriot-News columnist Paul Beers wrote in March 1982 of Mary's attitude toward charity. "It makes me feel more alive."

That was a line repeated through the years by other writers as well.

When the Lancaster Jewish Community Center named its new building after Mary in 1974, the press release sent out for the occasion cited still another Mary Sachs view of charity.

"She would say, 'Years ago, when I first decided to share, it was like getting out of prison. Through the years I have always found that I never gave anything away that I didn't get a great deal more in return. We are all here on Earth to do service, and we should be happy to do it."

Women's Wear Daily's Sam Feinberg shared yet another Mary Sachs epigram in his 1954 series of articles about the shop and its proprietor: "The only thing I have is what I give."

That Sachs philosophy was summed up in an old proverb cited in the 1970 program of the religious school building dedication service at Temple Ohev Sholom, endowed by the Trust she left behind: "What one tries to keep, he loses; what one gives away, he keeps forever."

Ten years later, Ohev Sholom Reform Temple honored Mary by naming its new Religious Education Building after her. A grant from the trustees of the Mary Sachs Trust contributed to the construction of the building.

In his sermon of dedication, according to *The Evening News* (September 5), Rabbi Emmet Allan Frank paid tribute to Mary Sachs as having emulated God. "Through her philanthropies," he said, "she has given to whom she loved. She has given that we might have a better knowledge of God."

Rabbi Frank also cited the biblical text, "Justice, justice shall you pursue" in reference to Mary's philanthropic legacy.

At the dedication of the Mary Sachs Religious Education Building, president of the congregation Bruce Cooper noted that "in a materialistic age, Mary Sachs was not a materialist. She did not want money for money's sake. To her wealth meant investing in others."

Sachs defined her charitable concepts in far greater detail in a 1953 letter to the Jewish community of Harrisburg on behalf of a fund-raising event for Israel. Through suffering at the time with shingles, she had accepted the chairmanship of the event, a concert by noted violinist Mischa Elman.

In the midst of a long letter asking others to give, Miss Sachs spelled out her philosophy of giving in depth. She wrote: "When there was a Hospital Drive, I did not ask, 'Will I benefit when I go to the hospital?' I hoped that I would never have to go there and am still hoping that I will never have to use a hospital, but I was happy to share in the drive.

"When there was a Community Welfare Drive, I was happy to share, and I am hoping that I will never (have) to ask for any benefits.

"When there is a Boy Scout Drive, you know that my sons will never be here for I am not blessed with a husband and I could not have sons legitimately.

"When the YMCA was built . . . I only asked, 'Will the Jew be welcome?'" And when the answer was yes, I gave a room in honor of a rabbi.

"When a chapel was built at Mercersburg, I gave an alms box in honor of a rabbi.

"I am simply outlining all these forces so as to enlighten you that my allegiance is not with the State of Israel only; it is with the State of Humanity-at-Large . . ."

This sense of noblesse oblige did not arrive only after success came to her. The instinct surfaced early in her life, when she was still working for others at low-wage jobs.

There is a story shared by then *Patriot-News* business editor Robert Evans in the mid-1960s about Mary that underscores this early trait.

"When a salaried employee, she had heard of destitute Polish children who needed help," Evans wrote. "She wanted to help but needed $100 for an appendix operation. She told the doctor she wanted to donate $25 but couldn't afford both that and the operation. 'Then we'll make the operation $75,' said the doctor."

Belated public recognition came for another early Mary Sachs gift in a scroll presented by the Boy Scouts to Mary, "whose very generous and timely gift assured the establishment of the (Hidden Valley) Boy Scout Camp at Loysville, Pennsylvania. Characteristic of the donor was her desire to remain unidentified at the time (1926); also her wish that no condition would be imposed upon acceptance of the gift other than this understanding: that it was made in honor of Rabbi Bookstaber, who had been a leader (in Boy Scout activities) in the Harrisburg area and elsewhere."

With the establishment of the State of Israel in 1948, Mary became the largest contributor in the Harrisburg area to help ease the new country's humanitarian problems.

Albert Hursh, executive directive emeritus of what was then called the Jewish Community Center and the United Jewish Community of Harrisburg, recalled Mary's efforts during that period with awe.

"She was quite a woman, and what she did was unheard of at that time," he reminisced. "She would pledge $50,000, $75,000, $100,000 and what she did to pay those pledges was rather unique. We'd have an Initial Gifts dinner for larger pledges at her home and bring in topnotch speakers. And Mary would make a little talk on her feelings and commitment toward Israel and then make her own pledge.

"The next morning, she'd call me in and hand me a check for the full amount. 'I borrowed the money from the bank,' she would say. 'I'll pay the interest. But the people in Israel need the money today.'"

She would do that every year, Hursh said.

"I'd tell this story at national conferences," he added, "and they would be amazed, but that's what she did."

Retired Harrisburg furniture dealer Richard Goldsmith confirmed that story and added one of his own.

"She was a great philanthropist, perhaps the only true philanthropist we ever had in this town, including anyone of us who gives a lot of money to charity," he said. "She would borrow the money. Harper Spong, president of Old Dauphin Deposit Bank, would lend her the money. Once, the old United Way, then called the Welfare Federation, was about to fail in its drive. Mary Sachs stood up at the meeting and said, 'It's not going to fail. Go out and work for two more weeks. Any money you don't collect, I will underwrite it; I'll make it good.'"

Frances Goldberg recalled that Mary challenged the men at those meetings.

The breadth of Mary's charitable contributions during her lifetime was staggering. The Harrisburg *Evening News* noted in an editorial, "Whenever there is a worthy community project to be completed or need to be met in this Capital City she can be found in the vanguard of its supporters."

The list of institutions helped during the heyday years of the Mary Sachs store is lengthy. To name but a few: A patient room in the cancer wing of Hadassah Medical Center in Jerusalem Hospital; Girl Scouts; Boy Scouts; Jewish National Fund; scholarships and other gifts to area colleges; American Cancer Society; First Pennsylvania "Woman of Valor" honored by the Israeli Government for promotion and purchase of Israel Bonds plus her direct charitable contributions to settle refugees in the Jewish State; American Red Cross; Holy Spirit Hospital Building Fund; and gifts to other area hospitals.

In addition, as mentioned, Mary was a Founder of the Albert Einstein College of Medicine at Yeshiva University in New York (Einstein recently became part of Montefiore Health System).

In his book, *City Contented, City Discontented*, about Harrisburg, writer Paul B. Beers included a chapter about Mary Sachs, whom he called "the city's savviest and most civilized entrepreneur." But, he added that "she [also] did her duty to bridge the gap" between the largely gentile community of Harrisburg and "the newly emerging, often professional Jewish community."

One stellar tribute came just a month before her death. At a dinner in Mary Sachs's honor on May 22, 1960, the Harrisburg Jewish Community Center named its auditorium for her. Mary accepted a plaque in her honor at a testimonial dinner that night. Henry H. Brenner was chairman of the Committee and Toastmaster, as described in the *Community Review*—the Jewish community paper—of May 27, 1960.

"It will be so in perpetuity," said Hursh, who was executive director then. "We could have raised $75,000 to $100,000 for that honor, but we wanted, by unanimous vote of the Board of Trustees, to dedicate it to her."

Mary's portrait gazes down from the rear wall of the room, and a plaque—bronze, with a bas-relief of Mary, reads:

THE MARY SACHS AUDITORIUM
DEDICATED TO A GREAT LADY
HUMANITARIAN
PHILANTHROPIST
Mary Sachs "Woman of Valor"
May 22, 1960

More than 350 people attended the Mary Sachs testimonial.

Mary even took out an ad headed: "With gratitude to all faiths for the night of my life," celebrating the Testimonial Dinner in her honor. It was attended, she noted, by representatives of the Protestant, Catholic, and other faiths as well as her own.

"It reminded me," Mary wrote, "that my own home was a sanctuary for women and men of all faiths in the Second World War . . ."

Indeed, commented Bern Sharfman, "Competitive weightlifters, no doubt, would have trouble hefting all of the plaques erected to Mary Sachs in this region before and after her death."

The ecumenical nature of her giving cut across communal and religious lines. It prompted such comments at her death as that by Bishop George Leech, then presiding over the Harrisburg Diocese of the Catholic Church: "The death of Mary Sachs is a distinct loss to our Harrisburg community. She has been a true friend and benefactor to all."

Mary's role of community benefactor did not end with her death. She left the residue of her estate, after some bequests to a few family members and key employees, to a charitable trust. The trust would be financed by store profits and by the revenues from the eventual sale of the shops.

The Trust has, through the years, continued to provide financial support to the causes locally and in Israel that Mary would have favored. It has been, in effect, a sort of mini-United Fund.

The Trust is composed of extended family members of Mary's as well as of leaders of the Jewish and general communities of the Harrisburg area.

They continue to fund the many causes with which Mary was affiliated.

EPILOGUE

Considering her accomplishments and the accolades she received for them, Mary Sachs is not as well known today as one would expect. In my research about Jewish women entrepreneurs outside central Pennsylvania, her name does not appear. Certainly, she is not as instantly recognizable a business and philanthropic leader as she once was.

Once, in addition to her portrait hanging at the JCC, her photograph also hung in the State Museum near the main circular entrance, along with those of other famous Pennsylvanians. Those photographs have been removed temporarily, but will be put back, according to Museum staff, in another part of the building at some point.

Recently, with the support of the Mary Sachs Trust, the awning at 208 North Third Street—the site of the original store—which had become dirty over time, was cleaned. The gold letters pronouncing that this was the Mary Sachs building are still present as well.

In a few obits in *The Patriot-News* lately, Mary's name and store were still invoked. For example: Hannah Edith Jacobs: Her employment history includes stints at the Mary Sachs Department Store, the Junior Dress Shop, and the Jack and Jill children's store. . . .

Joseph Romeo, 75, of Camp Hill, Pennsylvania, a U.S. Armed Forces veteran of the Korean War, a custom tailor for Mary Sachs in Harrisburg, Pennsylvania, died in Camp Hill on Saturday, October 18, 2003. . . .

Clearly, a person having been affiliated with the Mary Sachs stores in some way still has resonance, more than 50 years after her death.

In addition to the book and journalistic sources mentioned above, there are three central repositories of material about Mary and the stores in Pennsylvania's capital city: chiefly, the State Archives; the Historic Harrisburg Association; and the Historical Society of Dauphin County.

The State Archives description of its collection is as follows: Collection contains correspondence, writings, photographs, newspaper clippings, scrapbooks and philanthropic memorabilia of Mary Sachs, 1928-1960. Harrisburg philanthropist, owner of successful retail stores in Harrisburg and Lancaster, and founder of Albert Einstein College of Medicine at Yeshiva University, Mary Sachs (1888-1960) was active in such Jewish organizations as the United Jewish Appeal and Israel Bond Campaign. The collection includes, in addition to personal papers and photographs, business records covering the years 1932-1960 that contain correspondence from Eleanor Roosevelt, as well as a 1933 letter from President Franklin Roosevelt. Also present are minutes, reports, advertisements, and pension data for Mary Sachs Inc., 1960-1970. The photographs include both exterior and interior views of the Lancaster store taken in 1938, 1954, and 1956. The unpublished autobiographical articles, news clippings and a paper by Milton Bernstein entitled, "Study of a Creative Woman," (undated), provide background on Ms. Sachs's rise from humble beginnings as a nineteen year old Jewish immigrant factory worker to the status of a "Merchant Princess," as she was referred to in the Congressional Record (1958). Also found scattered through the file are photographs of African-American and Hispanic clerks and staff employed in the Lancaster and Harrisburg stores.

There are, of course, the memories of family members, friends, and patrons of the store. But many of the people who knew Mary or remember the store or both are gone.

Once in a while, too, there are surprises, such as this anonymous blog dated from October 16, 2012, on the online Department Store Museum:

"You should look into Mary Sachs in Harrisburg and Lancaster, PA. Unbelievably unique store!! Much better than Pomeroys or Hess. Pomeroys had great Christmas windows, and Hess had the restaurant with models. Mary Sachs in Harrisburg was better than Lancaster. Mary Sachs was by far the greatest shopping experience of my lifetime. The PA State Historic Museum did an entire exhibit about Mary Sachs. There has been a book written about Ms. Sachs and the stores. Thank you for the trip back Memory Lane."

One reason I wrote this book was to mitigate against the lack of or insufficient knowledge of Mary and her achievements. Another was to seek perhaps greater insights into what made her successful, even unique. But history has a way of discovering and rediscovering people. For example, it was gratifying to know that Open Stage of Harrisburg, in its second annual installment of "Stories from Home" (subtitled "City Beautiful," June 2013), production about the city and its history, included a monologue about Mary Sachs.

Appreciation is due to Anne Alsedek, who oversees the June production every year and is Open Stage's education director (and more), and to Linde Stern, a wonderful actor who brought the segment about Mary Sachs to life. (See *Mary Remembered*, page 95, and *Appendix I*, page 97.)

DOWNTOWN HARRISBURG DURING THE TENURE OF MARY'S STORE

For several years after World War II, the area was a bustling, busy city, according to Morton Spector. The population of the capital city was more than 90,000, and there were little or no shopping centers in the surrounding area. "Most retail activity was downtown," Spector said.

There were five movie theaters, as compared with today's none—and many clothing stores (whereas there are virtually none, today). There were many stores owned and operated by Jews, such as Davids for Men, Junior Dress Shop for Women, and Mary Sachs for Men, Women, and Children. There were two major hotels with excellent restaurants—the Penn Harris and the Harrisburger—and other coffee shops and drug stores, too.

At the time, the Commonwealth of Pennsylvania needed additional office buildings. But many downtown buildings housed these offices until the new buildings were built, Spector added. This meant a lot of people were already in the downtown areas.

Most of the streets were two ways, and parking was available on all streets, many without meters. No large parking garages were there.

Gradually, over the next few decades, as people who worked for the State moved to the new Capitol building and shopping centers were springing up (outside the inner city), the retail businesses suffered and closed up, one by one.

By this time Mary Sachs had died, and the store was sold, but it too, closed.

Downtown has never fully recovered, to this day, Spector lamented. It's an opinion shared by many—but of course, changes are forthcoming under the relatively new mayoral administration. One can hope.

MARY REMEMBERED

We've spoken before about how Mary Sachs is not as well known today as one would expect. Two events that occurred in just one week in November 2015 indicate that she is not forgotten.

MARY SACHS NOW OCCUPIED

Mary's residence, vacant for a number of years, is occupied again and referred to as the house of the entrepreneur-philanthropist.

Mike and Sally Wilson, who purchased it in an auction last year along with the next-door Ledgestone House at 2909 North Front Street, are now living on the second floor of the Mary Sachs House.

They have turned the Ledgestone into The Manor on Front, a bed and breakfast. A ribbon-cutting ceremony was held November 9, 2015, with Mayor Eric Papenfuse in attendance.

Meanwhile, the Wilsons are continuing to renovate the Mary Sachs House; the first floor will be used as additional B&B space.

"Originally we thought we'd live in the 2909 and rent out the Mary Sachs House as office space," said Mike Wilson, who had worked on the Ledgestone as a young man and dreamed of owning it. "But then it struck us that the Ledgestone is perfect as a B&B, and we will continue to live in the Mary Sachs."

As stated on B&B's web site (themanoronfront.com), the Ledgestone and the Mary Sachs both have been "beautifully renovated to showcase period details against a tailored, elegant interior, surrounded by a lush campus of mature trees with river views and gorgeous sunsets. The Ledgestone is a 1920s revival Tudor mansion, while The Mary Sachs is a colonial-style limestone mansion."

Registration for the B&B is at the office in the Mary Sachs House.

ICONIC MARY

The status of Mary Sachs as one of the Commonwealth's greats has again been confirmed in *Pennsylvania Icons*, an exhibit featuring a diverse array of artifacts from the collections of the State Museum of Pennsylvania and other Pennsylvania Historical and Museum Commission historic sites and museums.

Pennsylvania Icons, which opened November 8, tells the story of the Commonwealth, its people, and the role they played in shaping the nation.

The exhibit features a peau-de-soie sleeveless black evening dress and matching coat with rhinestone accents, which was sold at either the Harrisburg or Lancaster Mary Sachs store.

Appendix I

MARY SACHS, as presented in "Stories from Home: City Beautiful," a production drawn from the city's history by Open Stage of Harrisburg, June 2013.

Music: Jewish, Eastern European. A small immigrant girl appears in babushka, shawl, and shmata. She is carrying a small bundle. She looks around, overwhelmed but inspired. Actors move to her and remove her peasant clothes, slowly replacing them with new American clothing. She gradually becomes glamorous during the following speech. An older, well-dressed woman appears.

MARY SACHS: I left Lithuania in 1892 and came to this country with my family. Pogroms, violence, destruction; we were made to leave our homes. I was only four years old. We came to Baltimore, USA. I was always taught to work hard, to give back. A mitzvah is one of the most important things you can do. It's a good deed, but also an obligation. And if you have mazel—do you know what that is? Luck!— you'll be fine. My father was a peddler, and I suppose that was where I got my sense of business. He loved making deals, figuring things out. So did I! (She laughs) . . . I got my first job in a cigar factory in Baltimore. Oh, those men! I was very shy at first, but soon I got to know what each customer liked. Mr. Herman—he liked the stinky ones, but Mr. Krauss preferred the milder ones! Then my parents moved here. And I found a position in a candy store in Steelton, in Pennsylvania. Much sweeter than the cigars! I always liked clothing, though. Always. I liked beautiful clothes, clothes that had a unique and classic look about them. I began to dream of a store of my own—a place where ordinary people could be made to feel special. So I worked for Mr. Schleisner in his store in Harrisburg to learn the clothing business. I worked hard—I always worked hard. Long hours. I loved clothes. Loved them. But one day they came to me and told me that the store was being sold. And then they fired me. I had done nothing wrong. I felt worthless—for a day or two. Then I said to myself, "Mary—Maruska,"my father called me that—"You are better than this! Keep going!" Then: again mazel, I had made a connection with a gentleman, Mr. Lowengard, Mr. Harry Lowengard. He had come to Schleisner's several times with his wife, and I had told him then of my dream of having my own store. I didn't even think he had remembered! So we called a meeting together, and I told him that I wanted to open a women's clothing store that was totally unique. He had an empty floor on the street level of his building on North Third Street and he offered it to me—and a small loan! We opened the store on September 6, 1918. I had very little capital, but I made a decision right away. I would not buy from local sellers—I would go to New York City, to the Garment District, to buy my stock. I would go every two weeks or so with my sister Yetta. They were lovely outings, I can assure you. We went on the train. We would eat on the Lower East Side, wonderful food! Corned beef. Pickles, right from the barrel! There were so many Jewish people there that I felt at home. We bought lovely dresses and coats, beautiful coats. I didn't have a lot of money for inventory, so I made a plan: we kept the stock in the back, and each customer would be ushered into her own dressing room. My staff would then bring her flattering clothing and dress her from head to toe. Just like a movie star! The women loved it. Right here in Harrisburg. I made more than $200,000 my first year! I had arrived. Our store was not cheap, and I felt bad about that sometimes, but our clothes lasted. They were timeless, of the highest quality. Camel hair coats, suits, sweaters, hats, all with my own label carefully sewed in them. It was very busy on Third Street, so I thought: "Why not offer

free valet parking?" It was common sense and good business—and our customers appreciated it. And I took care
of my workers, too. I offered pensions to them; I wanted
them to be happy, so that they would do a good job. Common sense again, right? That's how I did things. All went
well for many years until one night in February 1931, when
the phone rang late at night: a fire had broken out in the
beauty shop, and the store burned to the ground. I wept.
I hadn't wept so hard since my father died. But after a period of mourning I said, "Mary, you must do this again." So
with the help of my family, my friends, my wonderful staff,
we rebuilt right down the block, bigger, better. Twenty-one
rooms now, and a men's shop! And the people came—they
kept coming and coming! *(She is delighted.)* But all along I
thought: "I must show my appreciation to this wonderful
place and the people who have been so good to me. I must
give back to this city. I must. It's a mitzvah." So I gave
money for scholarships, to the poor, to hospitals, to the
new State of Israel. Even to establish a Boy Scouts' camp.
Go to the auditorium at the Jewish Community Center. It
has my name. *(SLIDES: Mary Sachs building, images of the
store. She watches them.)* I am so proud that people will
remember me. I am so mazeldik. (She goes to the young
immigrant girl who has been dressed by the other actors.
She removes a brooch she has been wearing and pins it on
the girl.) Beautiful.

Appendix II

(From a school composition written by Leah Sacks, now Leah Sacks Hagelberg, 32, then a student at the Rabbi David L. Silver Yeshiva Academy in Harrisburg.)

My Dad's office used to be the home of Mary Sachs. She was a famous businesswoman. She helped a lot of people by donating money for charity. She was Jewish. Mary Sachs lived at 2917 North Front Street. There were many parties at her house. Famous people like Eleanor Roosevelt stayed there! Up to 16-20 soldiers stayed there at a time during World War II. Mary's house was very nice when she lived there. The floors were all black, and there were many fireplaces. There was a pink marble bathroom, and her room was pink. There was even a special music room for concerts. A cook and maid lived in the garage. It was very nice to live at Mary Sachs's house.

Mary Sachs's house is 60 year old and is now a law office for Smigel, Anderson, and Sacks.*

I chose Mary Sachs's house because it is my dad's office, and because Mary Sachs was a very special person.

Mary's help was felt in many places: the Museum for Scientific Discovery (now part of Whitaker Center for Science and the Arts); all area hospitals; at least seven area colleges; the secular and religious communities; and of course, her own Jewish charities at home and in Israel.

* Currently the law office is in another location.

Appendix III

Recent acquisitions in the exhibit include an 1839 woven coverlet from Hanover Township (this being three years before they were divided into East and West), a 1959 wedding dress from the Mary Sachs Shop, and numerous photographs including a portrait of Simon Cameron, the likeness of which is new to our collections. We received four volumes of photographs showing dozens of buildings in Dauphin County and throughout the east coast that were made from Hummelstown Brownstone Company. Women also have been added to our stacks, the AAUW having first donated their archives to HSDC in 2011.

(From *The Oracle*, publication of the Historical Society of Dauphin County, Summer 2013)

"Everybody has a Mary Sachs story to tell," said Peter Seibert, curator of the Dauphin County Historical Museum (February 1990)

ADDITIONAL BIBLIOGRAPHY

Marcus, Jacob Rader, ed., *The American Jewish Woman: A Documentary History* (1981).

Baum, Charlotte, Paula Hyman, and Sonya Michel. *The Jewish Woman in America* (1978).

Glenn, Susan A. *Daughters of the Shtetl: Life and Labor in the Immigrant Generation* (1990).

Hyman, Paula E. *Gender and Assimilation in Modern Jewish History: The Role and Representation of Women* (1995).

Joselit, Jenna Weissman. *The Wonders of America* (1995).

Todd M. Mealy, *Legendary Locals of Harrisburg* (2014).

www.ingramcontent.com/pod-product-compliance
Lightning Source LLC
Chambersburg PA
CBHW070833100426
42813CB00003B/605